Level A

THINKING CONNECTIONS

Concept Maps for Life Science

MW01267745

Frederick Burggraf

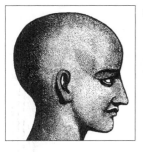

© 2001
CRITICAL THINKING BOOKS & SOFTWARE
P.O. Box 448 • Pacific Grove • CA 93950-0448
www.criticalthinking.com • Phone 800-458-4849 • FAX 831-393-3277
ISBN 0-89455-702-5
Printed in Canada

TABLE OF CONTENTS

INTRODUCTION

Background

Concept maps were first developed from the cognitive learning theory of David Ausubel in the 1960s and 1970s and later popularized by Joseph Novak and D. Bob Gowin in their book *Learning How to Learn*. Fundamental components of this work include the following ideas:

- Knowledge is constructed.
- The most important factor influencing learning is what the learner already knows.
- Concepts are the central elements in the structure of knowledge and the construction of meaning.
- Concept maps serve to externalize concepts and improve thinking.

As graphic organizers, concept maps show how concepts (things, ideas, objects, activities) are related or linked to each other. They are visual road maps of meaning and understanding.

Concept maps model how people think: in hierarchies, in propositions, in contexts, and with multiple cross connections. The human mind is amazingly adept in seeing relationships in unexpected and wondrous ways, and can slip in and out of contexts and hierarchies with astonishing ease. Mapping of concepts allows the "mapper" to represent his or her understanding accurately, including far-flung links. Out of all of this, the mapper will construct and clarify conceptual *meanings*.

Thus, the best concept maps are those that students generate by themselves. Each student has a slightly (or not so slightly) different view and grasp of the concepts, and those differences will show up on the maps students create. Student-generated maps are, therefore, unique and intensely personal, and have tremendous value to both the students (whose cognitions are represented) and to you (it gives you a direct look into each student's understanding).

Unfortunately, bringing students to the point where they can do their own accurate, readable maps requires time, instruction, and lots of practice (rare commodities in today's classrooms). The next best alternative is to use concept map exercises such as those found in this book. These exercises have solid educational value in concept clarification, content reflection, meaning building, and assessment and foster many of the same skills required to originate concept maps.

About These Exercises

The concept maps in Thinking Connections span 42 topics in elementary school life science. The topics were chosen using the National Science Education Standards as a guide.

The practice exercise on page 2 is a good introduction to concept mapping. It uses terms and concepts that should already be familiar to students. This exercise will give students the idea of what the tasks ahead will be in content-rich maps.

Concept maps can be used with a wide range of student abilities because they represent the individual understanding of the learner, regardless of his or her level. There are two levels for each map topic, addressing the needs of a broader population of students. The lower challenge map is designated by *two* small bars at the end of the title line; the higher-challenge map has *three* small bars at the end of the line.

Typically, lower-challenge maps have:

- more seed words,
- fewer technical words,
- shorter word lists,
- fewer connectors and simpler paths.

The presence of two levels of maps allows you to differentiate your assignment, even in the same class. It also allows these maps to be used across a wide spectrum of abilities and grade levels.

Structure, Features, and Notations of Concept Maps

Concept maps have three major components: items, connectors, and labels.

❑ *Items*—These are objects, ideas, places events, processes, and activities. Item names are placed in boxes in the concept map. The "main" item of a map is always shown in all capital letters. It sets the *domain*, or topic, of the map. Other items are lower case, showing subordinate relationships. Concept maps typically follow a top-down hierarchy of organization, with the main item being a general term and descending terms becoming increasingly specific. Students read maps intuitively this way, starting at the top and working downward. (Unfortunately, the limits of forcing a map onto one sheet of paper often compromise aspects of the hierarchy.)

☐ *Connectors*—Connectors are lines that join items, indicating which ones are related or linked and how they are linked. Connectors provide map syntax. The maps in the book were designed to be read from top to bottom (and, to a lesser degree, from left to right). The natural top-down flow eliminates the need for every connector to be an arrow.

☐ *Labels*—Labels are words associated with each connector. They show *how* items are related or linked.

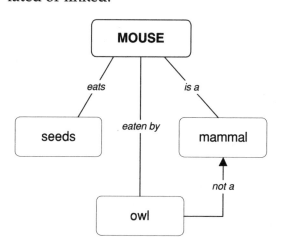

Figure 1. A simple concept map

The concept map in Figure 1 has four items. The lines that connect them are connectors. Each connector has a label showing the nature of the link.

Arrows

The natural flow of the concept maps in the book is top-down, left-to-right. In the map below, for example, it's obvious that the representation is that the vulture eats the raccoon.

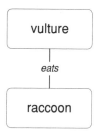

Figure 2. Top–down interpretation is intuitive

There are instances, however, where there is ambiguity about the direction of the relationship. For example, in Figure 3, do vultures eat (dead) raccoons or do raccoons eat vultures (eggs)?

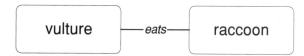

Figure 3. In some cases, interpreting relationships is difficult

Arrows show how to read the relationships and links. In Figure 4, the arrow makes it clear that, in this case, raccoons eat vultures.

Figure 4. Adding arrows simplifies interpretation

The Practice map (pg. 2) has three arrows; when you work that map with your class, discuss how the arrows show the direction of the relationships.

A map will sometimes close a loop by connecting widely separated portions of the map and bringing a relationship back to its beginning. Consider the following example:

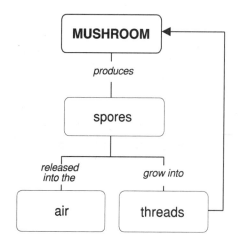

Figures 5. Closing a loop

In this example, notice the line from *threads* goes back to the main item. This line closes a "loop" in the map and shows how the *threads* relate not only to *spores* but also to new mushrooms.

Line Styles

The normal style of a connector is a solid line. A dotted line may be used to show a weaker, more tentative or less likely link.

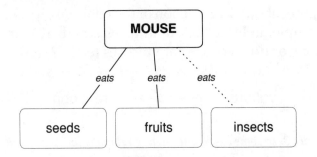

Figure 6. A dotted line shows a weaker link

For example, in Figure 6, a mouse is normally an herbivore but, in some rarer situations, may eat other animals. The dotted line shows this relationship.

A dotted line may be used to clarify relationships. In Figure 7, the connector *to* doesn't actually define the relationship, but rather clarifies the connector *attach*.

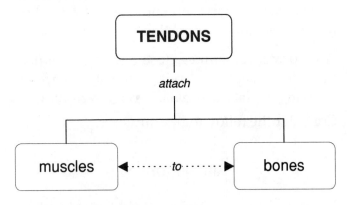

Figure 7. The dotted connector helps explain another connector

Multiple Connectors

Connectors can be joined to create multiple connectors. These usually take two forms:

1. The "fork" connector, branching out forklike under an item.

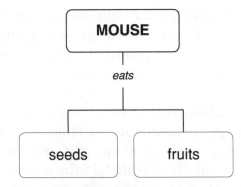

Figure 8. A "fork" connector

Notice how, in this case, the label *eats* appears only once and defines both relationships.

2. The "flag" connector, branching out on one side under an item.

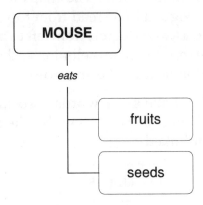

Figure 9. A "flag" connector

In both examples, the relationships are read as "and" relationships: "a mouse eats fruits *and* seeds."

Seed Items

All the maps in this book include a few "seed" items—words already placed in their correct locations on the map. Lower-challenge maps typically have more seed words than higher-challenge maps.

The seed words, in combination with surrounding connector labels, provide clues to get students started filling in the map. The map answer keys suggest good starting points.

Colors

A number of maps in this collection ask students to color certain items and then complete a Color Legend. This allows for another layer of information to be represented on the maps. Students will need highlighters, colored pencils, or crayons. Correcting mistakes made in coloring maps is difficult, so have spare maps handy.

Actually, any map can be made better with color, even if it's just to color in various branches to make them more distinguishable. Any time a student colors branches on a map, however, encourage him or her to make a Color Legend so that the meaning, no matter how simple, is clear.

Picture Galleries

At their very core, concept maps are graphic organizers, and the presence of drawings or other visual representation of concepts adds to their abilities to represent learning. Some of the maps in the book have collections of pictures for the student to place in the map.

Activities that involve graphics may require scissors and tape or glue in the classroom. Some students may balk at cutting out the graphics and taping or pasting them on the map, but later on, when it's time to use the map to review the topic, those graphics will make the map even more understandable and accessible.

Diagrams

Some of the maps in this book ask students to match parts of a diagram to individual items. Certain items have a box in one corner for the student to write a letter corresponding to a letter on the diagram.

The Concept Files

Concept Files are review summaries included in this book for each topic. The Concept Files cover topic background, vocabulary, major informational points, and other important data. Covering all the map content, Concept Files allow you to use all the maps in this book regardless of the curriculum you're using.

Using the Concept Files

If the curriculum you're using does not include all the concepts and vocabulary found on the map, give students the Concept File for the topic and let them use it as a study guide. Alternatively, you could provide other references and resources (textbooks, dictionaries, encyclopedias, etc.) so that students can look up the terms not in your course text.

The Concept File may make a good review sheet for a topic even if you don't use the concept map.

How to Use the Concept Map Exercises

Concept Maps are extremely versatile across a wide range of student abilities. Here are just a few suggestions for using these concept maps:

1. **As study aids**—Students who ask for extra help may benefit if they are given a map to complete while they read the source materials.

2. **As assessments**—Concept maps are excellent assessment tools and can be used to evaluate student understanding as well as the effectiveness of your teaching. Students who have a firm conceptual grasp of the material will usually do very well with the exercises. When a student has a lot of difficulty with a map, it usually indicates a lack of understanding of the material. (Oddly enough, students who do very well at memorizing may have trouble with concept maps. This is because these students have learned to do well by echoing back material without really understanding it.) If many students consistently show errors in one or more parts of a map, it may be a sign to go over the material again or in a different way.

3. **As review**—Before the end of a unit, use the concept map as a class activity for reviewing the lesson. Also, previously completed maps make great starting points as students study for large unit, semester, and course tests.

4. **As homework**—As students read new materials or study for review, concept maps can provide a focus activity and help the students graphically organize the content.

5. **As small-group activities**—Allowing students to work in groups of two or three can produce interesting and valuable interactions. You can allow students to use their textbooks and other references, or make the activity a closed-book exercise. (If you do allow references during map activities, you'll find that many groups will use these resources.) Typically, students will plan together and consider various possibilities for completing the map. It's very common to hear students arguing points of concept placement and the logic behind them. Stu-

dents also get intense practice with vocabulary during these sessions. Most importantly, the *meaning* and *understanding* of concept becomes paramount; it isn't that they just *use* the words and ideas, but rather the map helps them *construct* meaning and understanding.

One strategy that can get students intensely involved is to correct a group's map right away and say, "There are [some number] items incorrect, but I'm not going to tell you which ones. Keep working." The students will go back and attack the map with new vigor, new arguments, and new thinking.

6. **As portfolio materials**—If you're using portfolio assessment, the concept maps that students complete are great additions to the materials you or the student chooses to put in the portfolio.

7. **As parts of tests**—If your students have not used a map as another activity, you could attach it to a chapter or unit test.

8. **As writing exercises**—Once students complete their maps, ask them to write a paragraph using the map as a guide. Items in the map will usually become subjects and objects of the sentences; connector labels will be used as the verbs.

About the Author

Frederick Burggraf began his career as a high school science teacher, teaching two years in western Pennsylvania and ten years in southern Maryland. In the early 1980s, he left the classroom and devoted his full-time efforts to developing educational software. He has authored over 40 software titles published by three national software houses. Mr. Burggraf is currently a specialist in verbal and visual communications, as well as an educational consultant. He has a B.S. from Indiana University of Pennsylvania (1970) and an MEd from the University of Maryland (1983).

THE PRACTICE MAP

In the map exercises in this book, students will be asked to fill in missing items from a list. They may also be asked to supply connector labels, complete a map legend, match items with a diagram, or cut out and affix images on the map.

The first map in this book is a practice map and serves to introduce your students to concept mapping and several features of these exercises. Many students take readily to concept maps, intuitively knowing what to do. But others have trouble with them, especially at first. The practice map can clear up many questions if you take some time to work the map with the class.

Strategy

Here is one strategy for using the Practice Map:

1. Pass out the map and use an overhead transparency on a projector as you work through it.

2. Suggest that the students look over the entire map to see all its aspects and what is included. Have them read *all* the connectors and terms in the word list. Point out that there are also graphics to place in the map. *It's this "big picture" approach that some students miss and is vital to completing concept maps successfully.*

3. Have students cut out the graphics before they start filling in the map.

4. Ask students for suggestions on where to start. More important, *ask them how they came up with those suggestions.* In other words, find out what strategies they used to attack the map. If students need a jump start, ask them to notice the item *water*. Ask, "What on the list or in the pictures is related to water?" The picture of the *canoe* is the only candidate. Now ask, "What powers a canoe?" After students have filled in the item *person*, have them notice the arrow pointing to *person*, connecting back with another *powered by* connector. Ask, "What else is powered by a person?" Then, let them go for a while.

This process is typical in completing concept map exercises. Often, students begin on items near the bottom of the map (where the hierarchy is most specific) and then move up the map, checking against other connectors and item names. Although some items can be placed in several spots on the map, there's only one way that all the items fit together.

5. When the items are all placed, it's time to color the map. Students should use highlighters, crayons, or colored pencils—if you can't provide these, ask the students the day before to bring them in.

The topic of this map, "Means of Transportation," was chosen for its familiarity—students can concentrate on the dynamics of the map and not struggle with the conceptual content.

The answer key for the practice map has many other suggestions for its use.

Concept Map: Practice!

Directions: Select words from the word list and fill in the blank map items. Use each word only once, and use all the words on the list. Cut and paste (or tape) the pictures in the correct boxes on the map. Then use highlighters, colored pencils, or crayons to color items that (1) have wheels and (2) are living. Show your color scheme in the legend.

Name _____

Date _____

Period _____

WORD LIST

air
bicycles
carts
engine
land
person
trucks

COLOR LEGEND

☐ Has wheels

☐ Is living

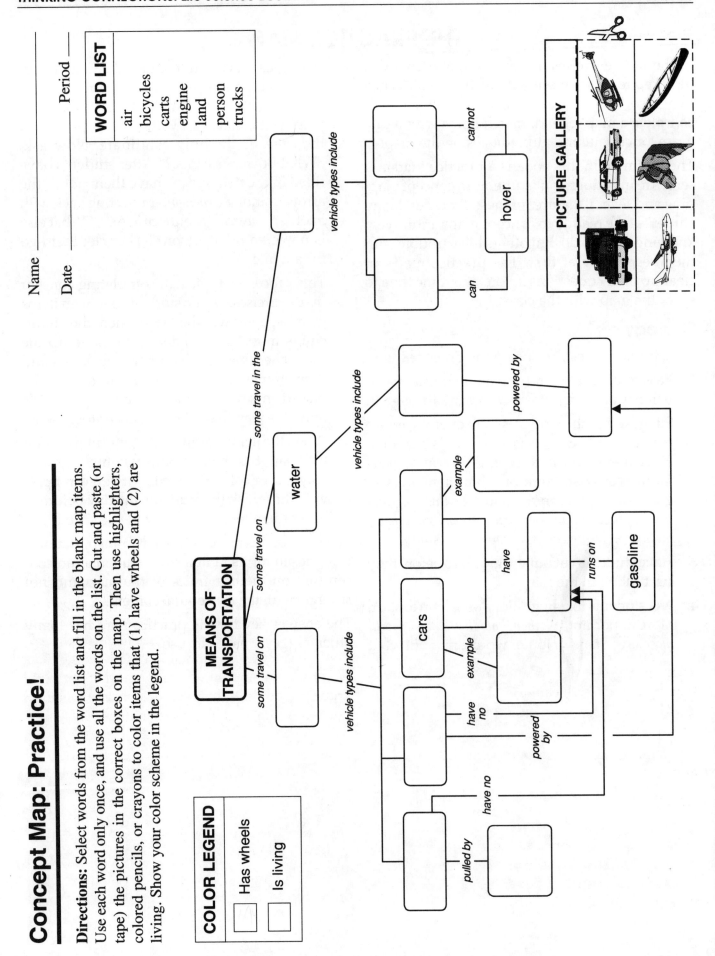

PICTURE GALLERY

MEANS OF TRANSPORTATION

some travel in the

some travel on

some travel on

vehicle types include

vehicle types include

vehicle types include

water

cars

hover

cannot

can

powered by

example

have

runs on

gasoline

example

have no

powered by

have no

pulled by

Answer Key

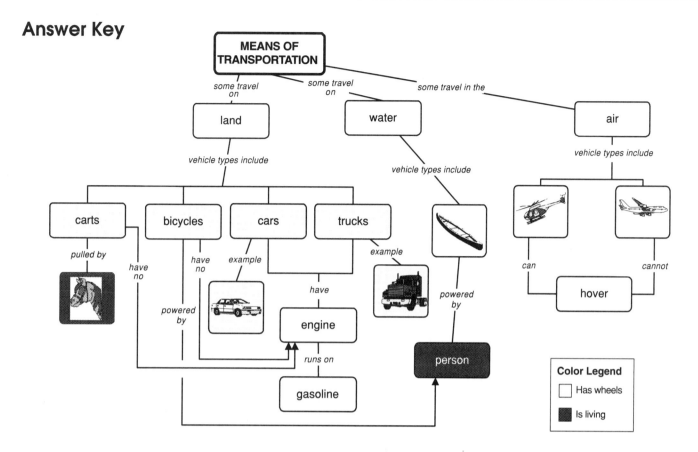

Teaching Suggestions

This practice map gives students experience working with a map where most of the information required is common knowledge. The map also introduces several of the map features found in this book.

Starting Hints

Students should first complete the map using the word list and the pictures. The item *water* is a good starting point because there's only one picture of a water vehicle (the canoe).

Some students may focus on the word list and forget that the pictures are choices for items in the map. In this map, square items hold pictures and rectangular items hold text.

Notes

Carts and the horses that pull them may be unfamiliar to some students. Including these items in the map was intentional; in many cases, students will have to finish maps by the process of deduction, finding a "best fit" for the items left over.

Once the maps are complete, you may want to check them for accuracy before you direct the students to color them. (Incorrectly colored items are hard to correct.)

Students should use one color to indicate those items that have wheels. These items are: carts, bicycles, cars, trucks, sedan (pictured), and semi (pictured). The picture of the jet was not included in this category because its wheels are not the primary method of movement. Nonetheless, it *does* have wheels, and some students may correctly argue the point. If they do, welcome it; this is an important part of the process of mapping—argument, defense, insight, and revision. That students are arguing a point and defending it is far more important as a critical thinking skill than getting the "correct answer."

Students should use a second color to indicate the items that are living. In this case, there are two: horse (pictured) and *person*.

A small number of students have serious difficulty with concept maps; this practice map should reveal who those students are and where they have problems.

Concept Map: Vascular Plants

Name _____

Date _____   Period _____

Directions: Select words from the word list and fill in the blank map items. Use each word only once, and use all the words on the list. Cut out the pictures and paste or tape them in the correct boxes.

WORD LIST

conifers	tubes
flowering plants	vascular tissue
roots	water
stems	

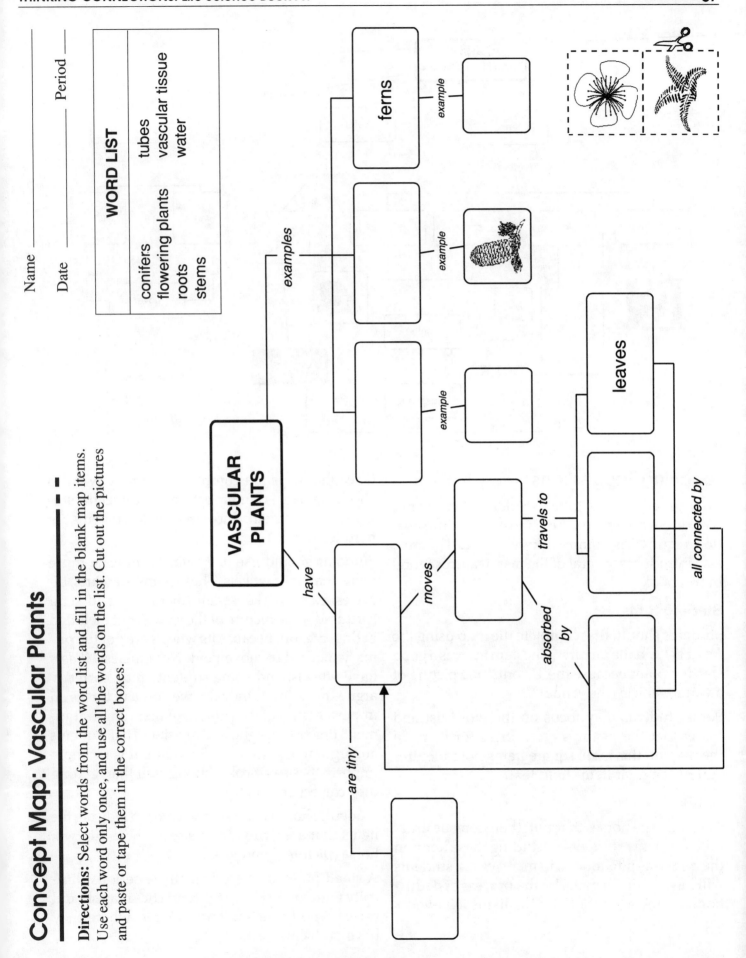

Name _____

Date _____

Period _____

Concept Map: Vascular Plants

Directions: Select words from the word list and fill in the blank map items.
Use each word only once, and use all the words on the list.

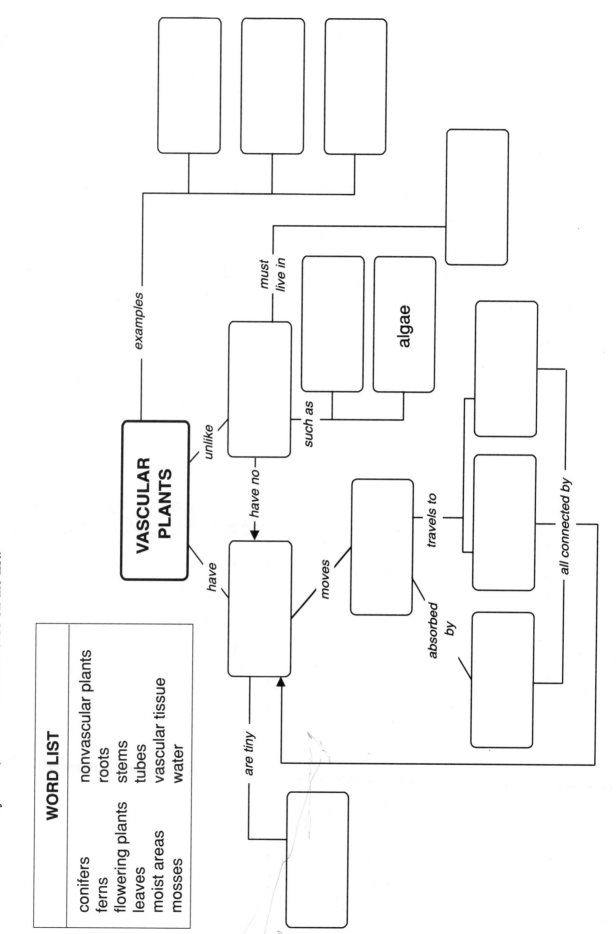

WORD LIST

conifers	nonvascular plants
ferns	roots
flowering plants	stems
leaves	tubes
moist areas	vascular tissue
mosses	water

Critical Thinking → C NCEPT FILE

Vascular Plants

Characteristics

Vascular plants have vascular tissue.

They can live in areas where nonvascular plants can't live.

They include

- conifers
- ferns
- flowering plants

Vocabulary

☐ **conifer**—evergreen plant with needle-shaped leaves

☐ **nonvascular plant**—a plant that does not have vascular tissue. These include mosses and algae. Because they can't move water very well, they must live in wet areas.

Vascular Tissue

Vascular tissue has cells that form tiny tubes.

These tubes move water from the roots to the stems and the leaves.

VASCULAR PLANTS

Lower Challenge

Score: 9 (7 words and 2 pictures)

Starting hints: The connector *absorbed by* suggests roots. The connector *are tiny* suggests tubes.

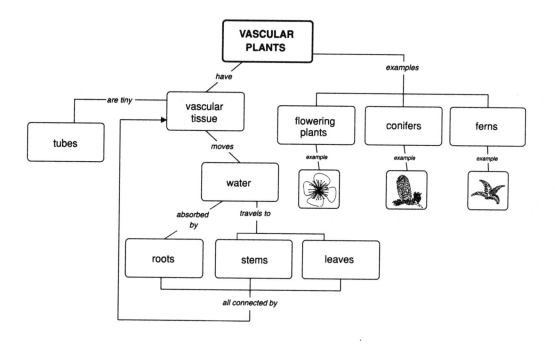

Higher Challenge

Score: 12 words

Starting hints: The connector *absorbed by* suggests roots. The connector *are tiny* suggests tubes.

The seed item *algae* is an example of a nonvascular plant.

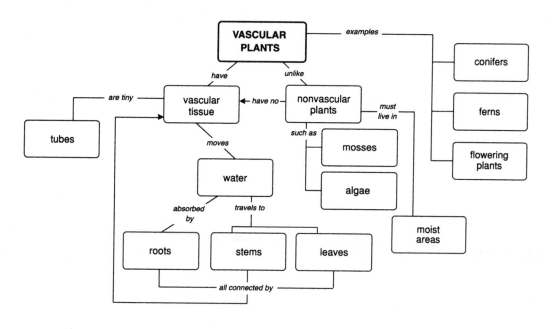

Concept Map: Plant Parts

Directions: Select words from the word list and fill in the blank map items. Use each word only once, and use all the words on the list.

Name _____

Date _____

Period _____

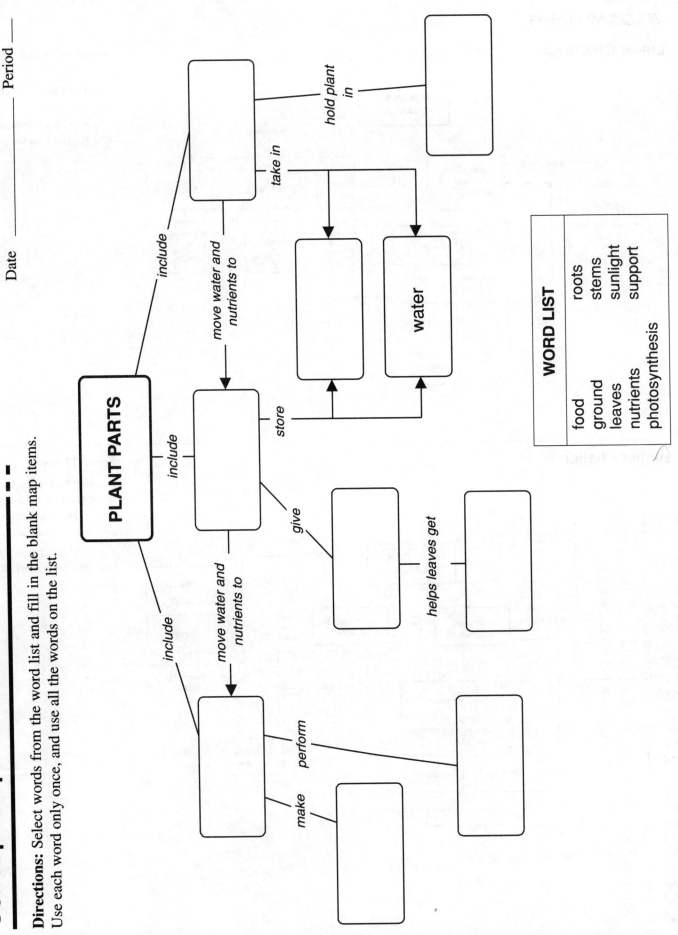

WORD LIST

food   roots
ground   stems
leaves   sunlight
nutrients   support
photosynthesis

Concept Map: Plant Organs

Directions: Select words from the word list and fill in the blank map items. Use each word only once, and use all the words on the list.

Name _____

Date _____ Period _____

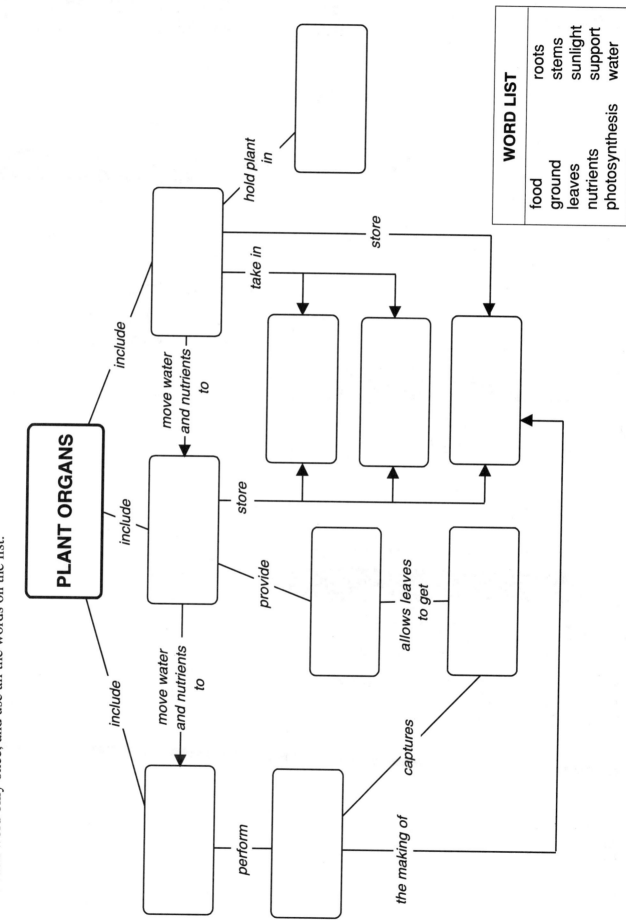

WORD LIST

food
ground
leaves
nutrients
photosynthesis

roots
stems
sunlight
support
water

Critical Thinking →

Plant Parts

Stems

- give the plant support
- help the leaves get sunlight
- move nutrients and water to the leaves
- store food and water

Leaves

- make food through the process of photosynthesis
- receive water and nutrients from the stems

Roots

- take in water and nutrients and move them to the stem
- hold the plant in the ground
- store food

Vocabulary

- ❑ **nutrients**—minerals and other chemicals that help plants grow
- ❑ **photosynthesis**—the chemical action where plants capture the sun's energy and make food

PLANT PARTS

Lower Challenge

Score: 9 words

Starting hints: The connectors *make* and *perform* on the left suggest the leaf, the factory of the plant.

The connector *take in* on the right suggests the roots.

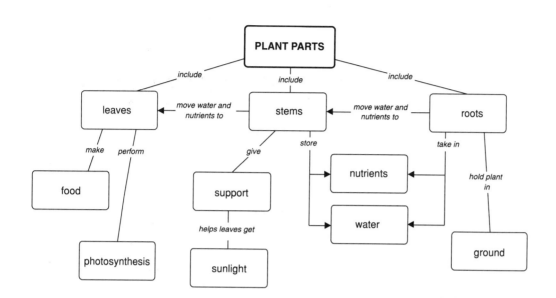

Higher Challenge

Score: 10 words

Starting hints: See notes above.

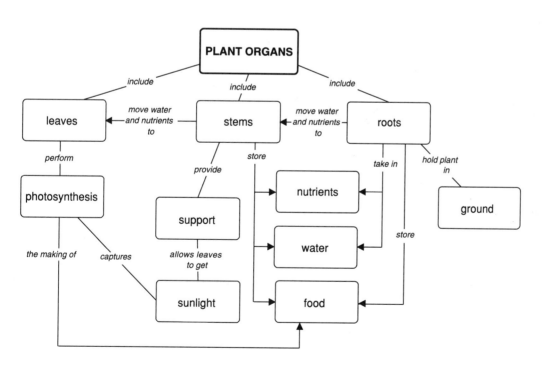

Name _____

Period _____

Date _____

Concept Map: Parts of the Root

Directions: Select words from the word list and fill in the blank map items.
Use each word only once, and use all the words on the list.

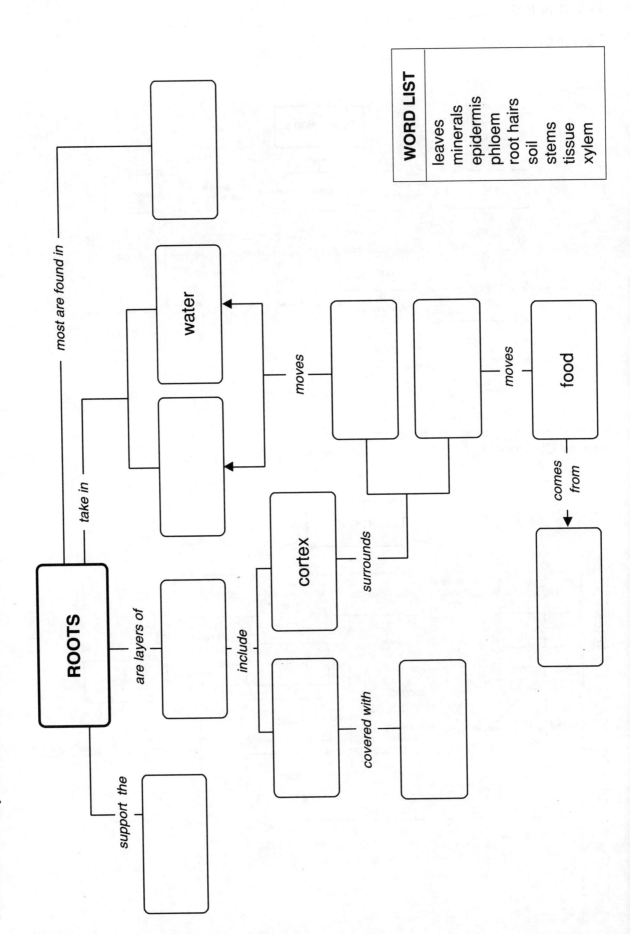

WORD LIST

leaves
minerals
epidermis
phloem
root hairs
soil
stems
tissue
xylem

Concept Map: Parts of the Root

Directions: Select words from the word list and fill in the blank map items. Use each word only once, and use all the words on the list. Then color your map using the color key.

Name _____

Date _____

Period _____

WORD LIST

cambium	root cap
cortex	root hairs
epidermis	soil
nutrients	surface area
phloem	water
protection	xylem

COLOR LEGEND

☐ tissues of the root

☐ materials that move through the root

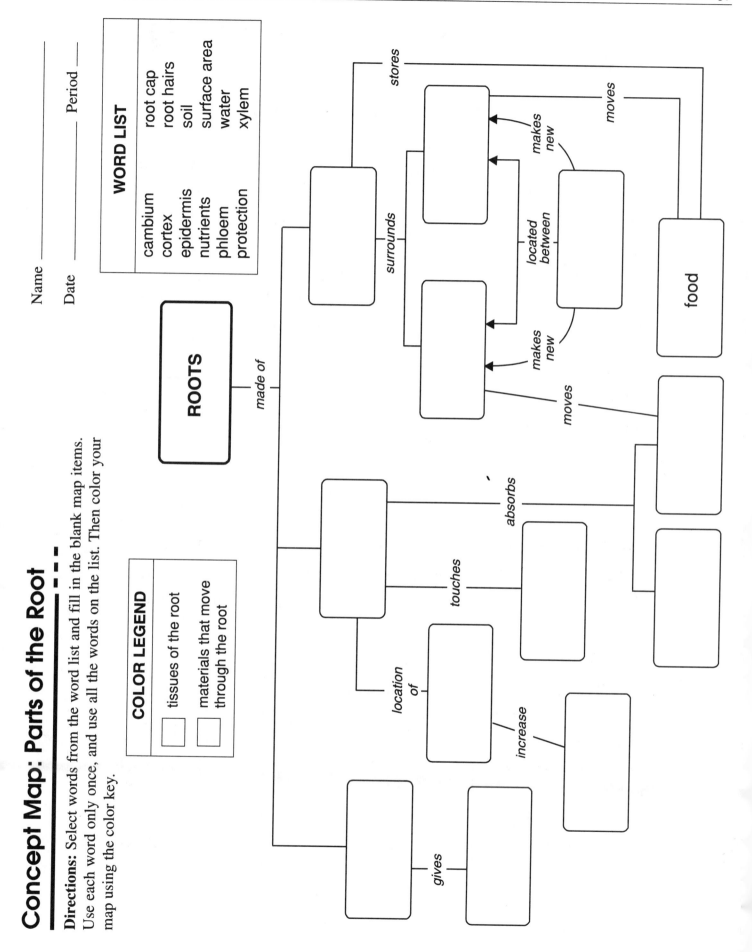

ROOTS

made of

stores

moves

makes new

located between

surrounds

makes new

makes new

moves

food

absorbs

touches

location of

increase

gives

Critical Thinking ➔  **C NCEPT FILE**

Parts of the Root

Main Tissues of the Root

Roots take in minerals and water. The root has six main layers of tissue:

- epidermis
- root cap
- cortex
- xylem
- phloem
- cambium

Vocabulary

❏ **epidermis**—the outer layer of the root

❏ **food**—energy-rich materials in the plant, made mostly in the leaves

Cambium

- found between the xylem and the phloem
- makes new xylem and phloem as the root grows

Cortex

- stores food
- central part of the root
- surrounds the xylem and phloem

Epidermis

- touches the soil
- covered with root hairs which make the surface area larger

Phloem

- moves food through the plant
- found in the cortex

Root Cap

- found at the tip of the root
- protects the root

Xylem

- moves water and minerals through the plant
- found in the cortex

PARTS OF THE ROOT

Lower Challenge

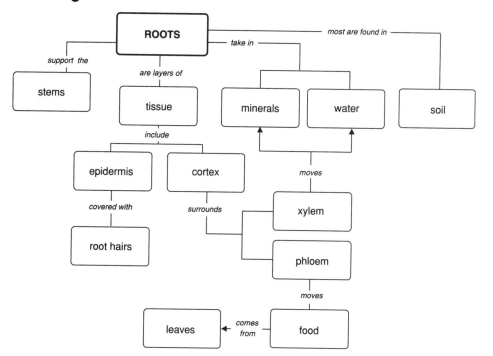

Score: 9 words

Starting hints: The connector *moves* (just right of center) pointing up to *water* suggests the item *xylem* below it. Similarly, the connector *moves* pointing to *food* suggests *phloem*.

Higher Challenge

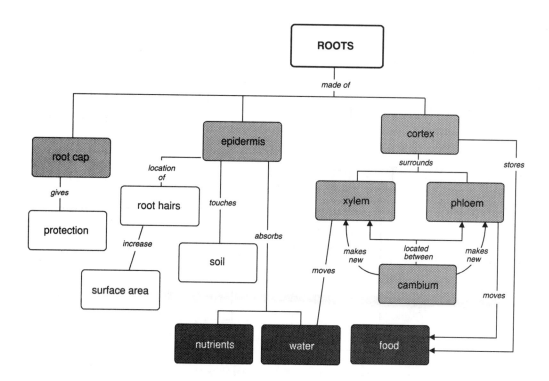

Score: 21 (12 words and 9 correct color placements)

Starting hints: The item *food* at the bottom right is connected to two other items. The connector *moves* suggests *phloem* and the connector *stores* points to *cortex*.

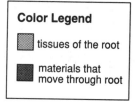

Color Legend

tissues of the root

materials that move through root

Concept Map: Root Systems

Directions: Select words from the word list and fill in the blank map items. Use each word only once, and use all the words on the list.

Name _____

Date _____

Period _____

WORD LIST

above ground	fibrous roots
aerial root	main root
beets	maple tree
branching roots	taproot
carrots	top of the soil

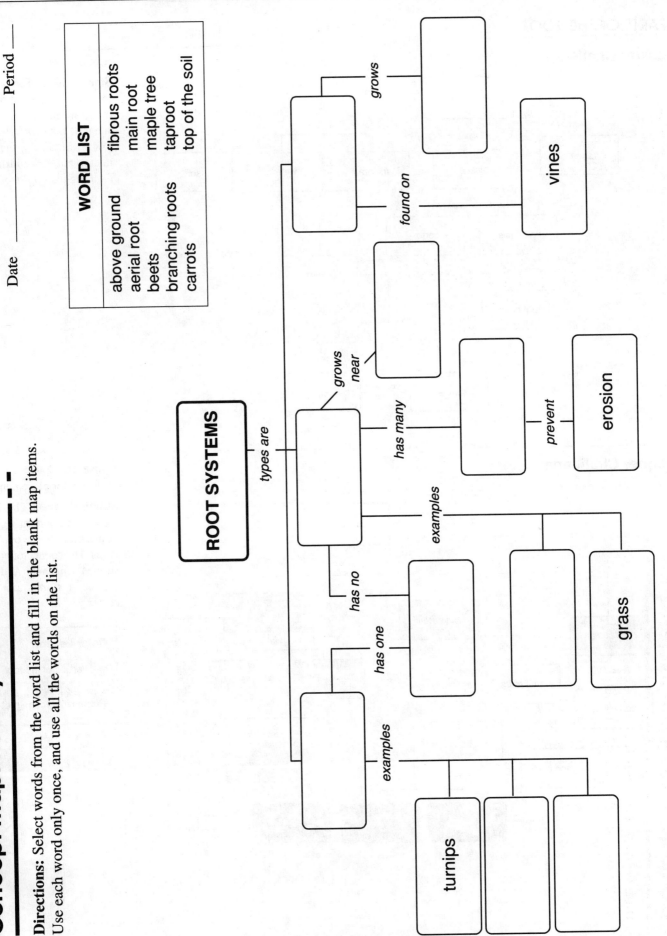

Concept Map: Root Systems

Directions: Select words from the word list and fill in the blank map items. Use each word only once, and use all the words on the list.

Name _____

Date _____ Period _____

WORD LIST

above ground
aerial root
beets
branching roots
carrots
erosion
fibrous root
food

grass
main root
maple tree
pine tree
smaller side roots
taproot
top of the soil
vines

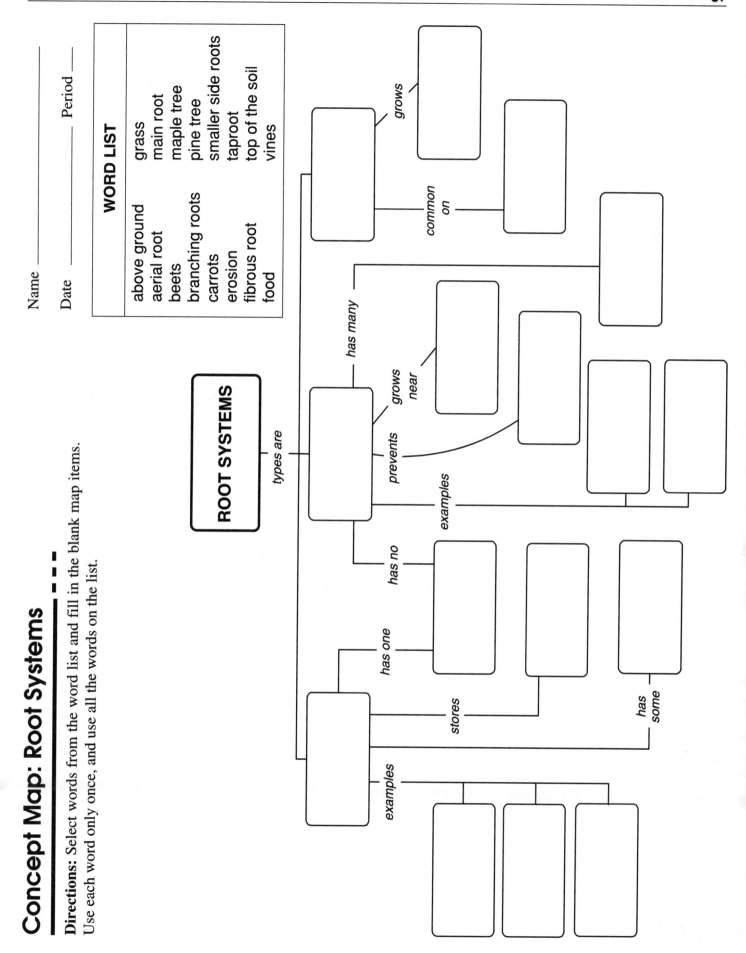

ROOT SYSTEMS

types are

grows

common on

has many

grows near

prevents

examples

has no

has one

stores

has some

examples

Critical Thinking → C🔆NCEPT FILE

Root Systems

Vocabulary

❏ **aerial**—related to the air, living out of the ground

❏ **erosion**—loss of soil due to water or wind

❏ **fibrous**—having fibers or threadlike structures

❏ **taproot**—a single large root

Types of Root Systems

Fibrous Roots	Aerial Roots	Taproots

• have no large, main root
• have many branching roots
• grow near the top of the soil
• help stop erosion
• examples are
  – maple tree
  – grass
	• grow above the ground
	• common on vines and other climbing plants
		• have one large, main root
		• store food for the plant
		• have smaller side roots
		• examples are
		  – turnips
		  – radishes
		  – beets
		  – pine trees
		  – carrots

ROOT SYSTEMS

Lower Challenge

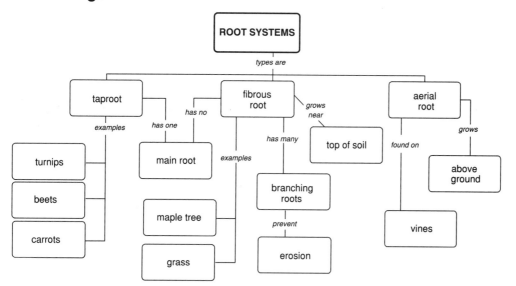

Score: 10 words

Starting hints: The item *erosion* refers back to *branching roots*. The seed item *turnips* refers back to taproot.

Higher Challenge

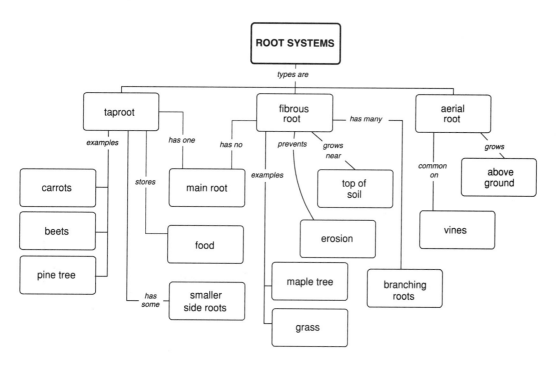

Score: 16 words

Starting hints: The connector *stores* on the left side of the map refers to taproot. The connector *prevents* has only one logical match in the word list; you might ask students what in the word list could be preventable (*erosion*), and then what type of root prevents it.

Name _____

Date _____

Period _____

Concept Map: The Stem

Directions: Select words from the word list and fill in the blank map items. Use each word only once, and use all the words on the list.

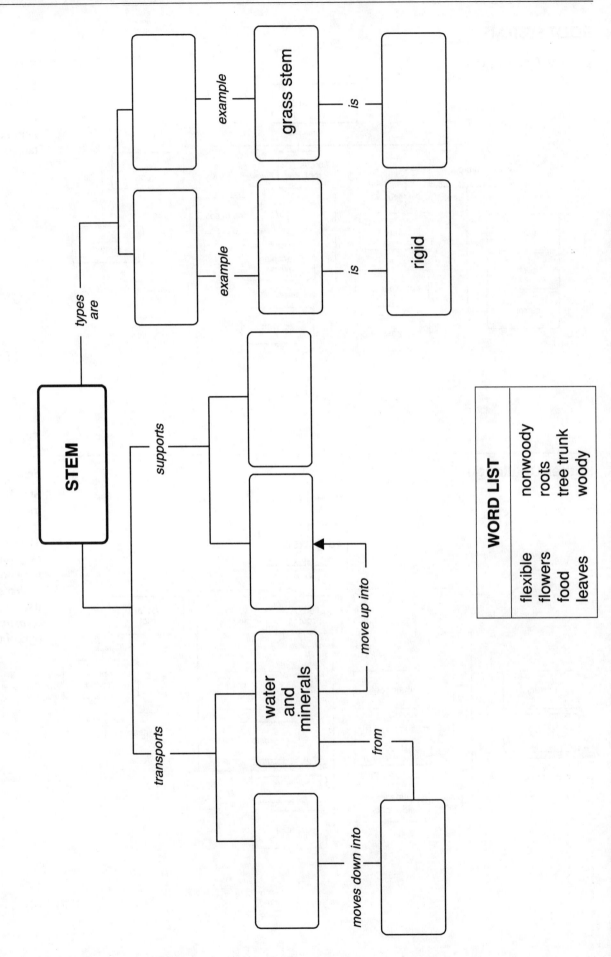

WORD LIST	
flexible	nonwoody
flowers	roots
food	tree trunk
leaves	woody

Name _____

Date _____

Period _____

Concept Map: The Stem

Directions: Select words from the word list and fill in the blank map items.
Use each word only once, and use all the words on the list.

WORD LIST

flexible	rigid
flowers	roots
food	tree trunk
grass stem	water
leaves	woody
nonwoody	years
phloem	xylem

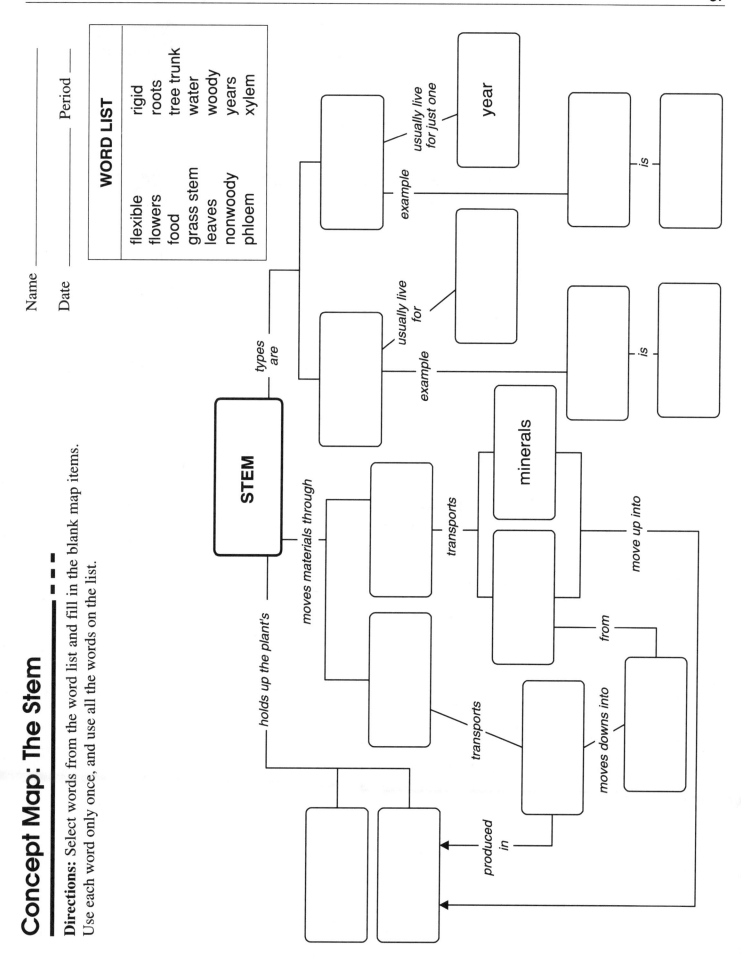

Critical Thinking → C⚲NCEPT FILE

The Stem

Functions

- Holds up the leaves and flowers.
- Moves materials
  - water
  - food (sugar)
  - minerals

Vocabulary

- ❏ **herbaceous**—another name for a nonwoody stem
- ❏ **phloem**—tissue that moves food down from the leaves to the root
- ❏ **xylem**—tissue that moves water and minerals up from the root to the leaves

Types

Woody stems
- usually live for many years
- are very rigid
- example is a tree trunk

Nonwoody stems
- usually live just one year
- are flexible
- example is a grass stem

THE STEM

Lower Challenge

Score: 8 words

Starting hints: The connector on the left, *transports*, and the seed item *water and minerals* point to the item *food*.

The seed item, *grass stem*, indicates a *nonwoody* stem.

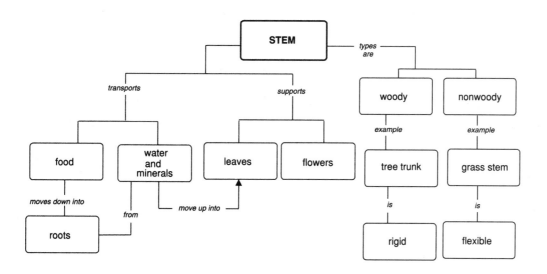

Higher Challenge

Score: 14 words

Starting hints: The connector on the left, *transports*, points to food.

The connector-item combination, *transports minerals*, indicates the item *xylem*. The seed item *year*, on the right, points to nonwoody.

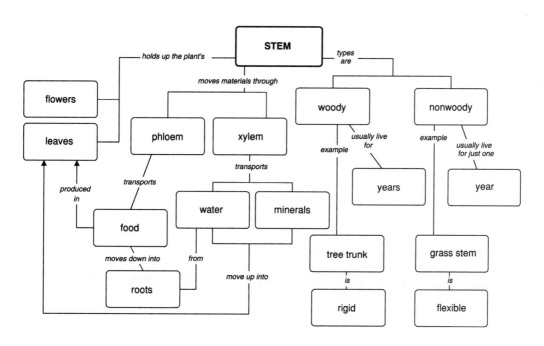

Concept Map: The Leaf

Name _____

Date _____ Period ____

Directions: Select words from the word list and fill in the blank map items. Use each word only once, and use all the words on the list.

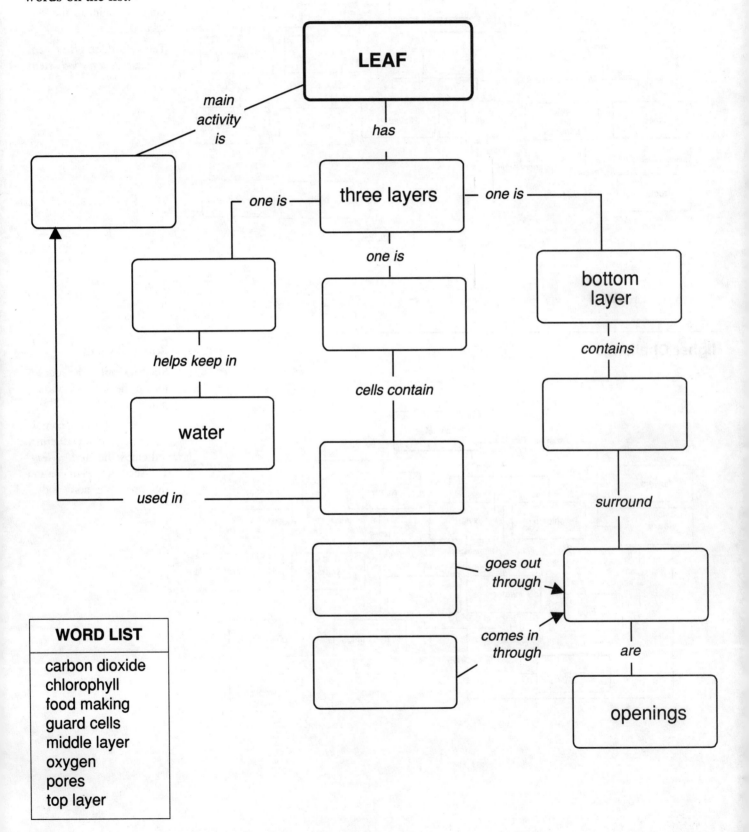

WORD LIST

carbon dioxide
chlorophyll
food making
guard cells
middle layer
oxygen
pores
top layer

Concept Map: The Leaf

Name _____

Date _____ Period _____

Directions: Select words from the word list and fill in the
blank map items. Use each word only once, and use all the
words on the list.

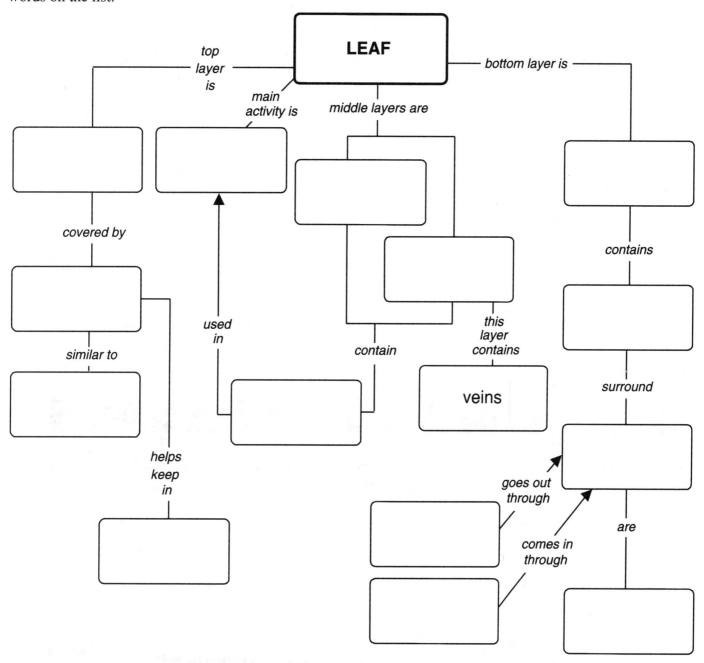

WORD LIST		
carbon dioxide	openings	stomata
chlorophyll	oxygen	upper epidermis
cuticle	palisades cells	water
guard cells	photosynthesis	wax
lower epidermis	spongy cells	

Critical Thinking →  CONCEPT FILE

The Leaf

Function

The leaf is the food factory of the plant.

The leaf makes the food by the process of photosynthesis. Photosynthesis takes place in the chloroplasts of the leaf cells.

Vocabulary

❑ **chlorophyll**—a green pigment used in photosynthesis

❑ **chloroplast**—cell that contains chlorophyll

❑ **cuticle**—a waxy material on the top layer of a leaf

❑ **epidermis**—the outermost layer of cells

❑ **stomata**—pores (openings) in the bottom layer of the leaf

Layers

Top Layer

The top layer of the leaf is the upper epidermis.

It is covered by a waxy cuticle, which helps keep water in the leaf.

Middle Layer

The middle layer is in the center of the leaf. It has two parts:

• palisades layer
• spongy layer, which contains the veins of the leaf

The middle layer has cells that contain chlorophyll.

Bottom Layer

The bottom layer is the lower epidermis.

It has pores called stomata. Each pore has guard cells that surround it.

Carbon dioxide enters the leaf through the pores. Oxygen is released through the pores.

THE LEAF

Lower Challenge

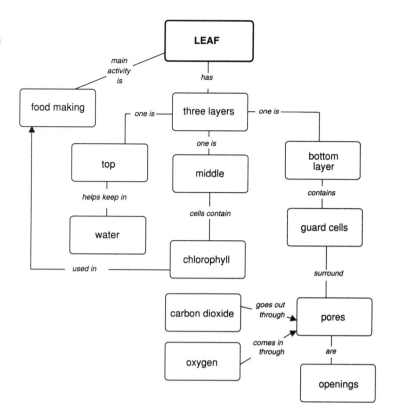

Score: 12 words

Starting hints: The items *top layer*, *middle layer*, and *bottom layer* were intentionally kept at the same level on the map.

The item at the bottom right, *openings*, describes *pores*.

Higher Challenge

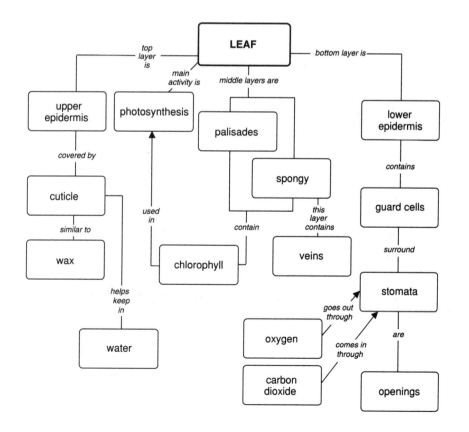

Score: 14 words

Starting hints: The seed item in the center, *veins*, is found in the spongy layer.

The connector on the right, *surround*, points to guard cells.

Concept Map: Plant Reproduction

Directions: Select words from the word list and fill in the blank map items.
Use each word only once, and use all the words on the list.

Name _____

Date _____

Period _____

WORD LIST

embryo	pollen grain
female sex cell	pollen tube
fertilized egg	rain
insects	seed
male sex cell	wind
ovule	

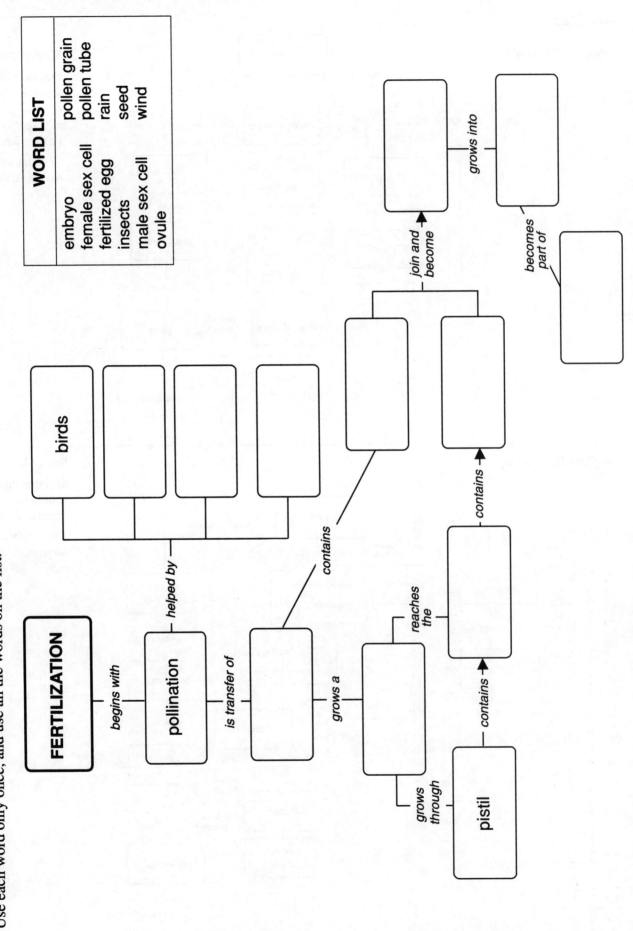

Concept Map: Plant Reproduction

Directions: Select words from the word list and fill in the blank map items. Use each word only once, and use all the words on the list.

Name _____

Date _____ Period _____

WORD LIST

birds
egg
embryo
female sex cell
insects
male sex cell
ovary
ovule
pistil
pollen grain
pollination
rain
seed
wind

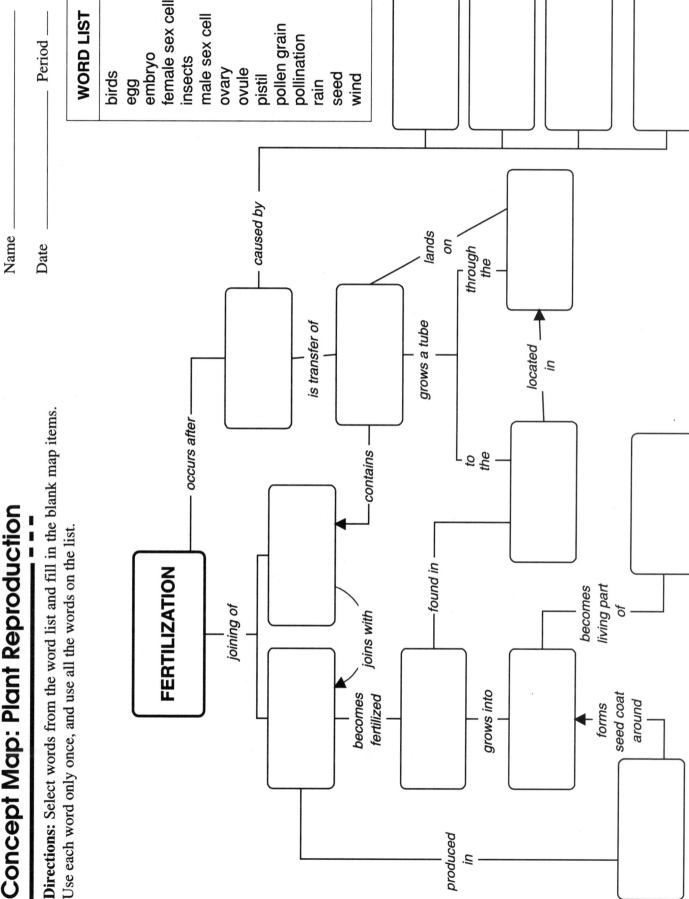

Critical Thinking →

Plant Reproduction

Pollination

Pollination happens when a pollen grain lands on the pistil of the flower.

Pollination can be helped or caused by:

- birds
- rain
- wind
- insects

The pollen grain grows a pollen tube through the pistil and into the ovule.

Vocabulary

- ❑ **female sex cell**—a small female cell (egg) that grows in the ovary of the flower
- ❑ **male sex cell**—a tiny male cell found in the pollen grain
- ❑ **pollination**—the transfer of a pollen grain onto the pistil of the flower

Fertilization

During fertilization, the male sex cell (in the pollen tube) joins with the female sex cell (in the ovule of the flower).

- This new cell becomes the fertilized egg.
- The fertilized egg grows into an embryo. The ovule grows a protective seed coat around the young embryo.
- The embryo becomes a part of the seed.

PLANT REPRODUCTION

Lower Challenge

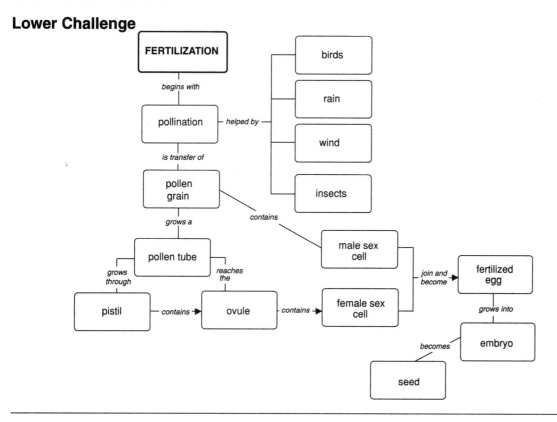

Score: 11 words

Starting hints: The connector at the right center, *join and become*, strongly point to the item *fertilized egg*. Working backwards reveals the items *male sex cells* and *female sex cells*.

The various helps to pollination can be listed in any order.

Higher Challenge

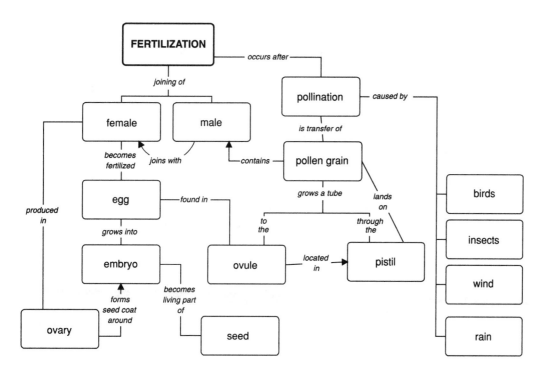

Score: 14 words

Starting hints: The curving connector, *joins with*, suggests a combining of sex cells.

The agents of pollination on the extreme right can be listed in any order.

Name _____

Date _____   Period _____

Concept Map: The Flower

Directions: Select words from the word list and fill in the blank map items. Use each word only once, and use all the words on the list. Place the letters from the diagram in the correct boxes on the map.

WORD LIST

bright colors	pistil
insects	pollen
ovary	sepals
petals	stamen

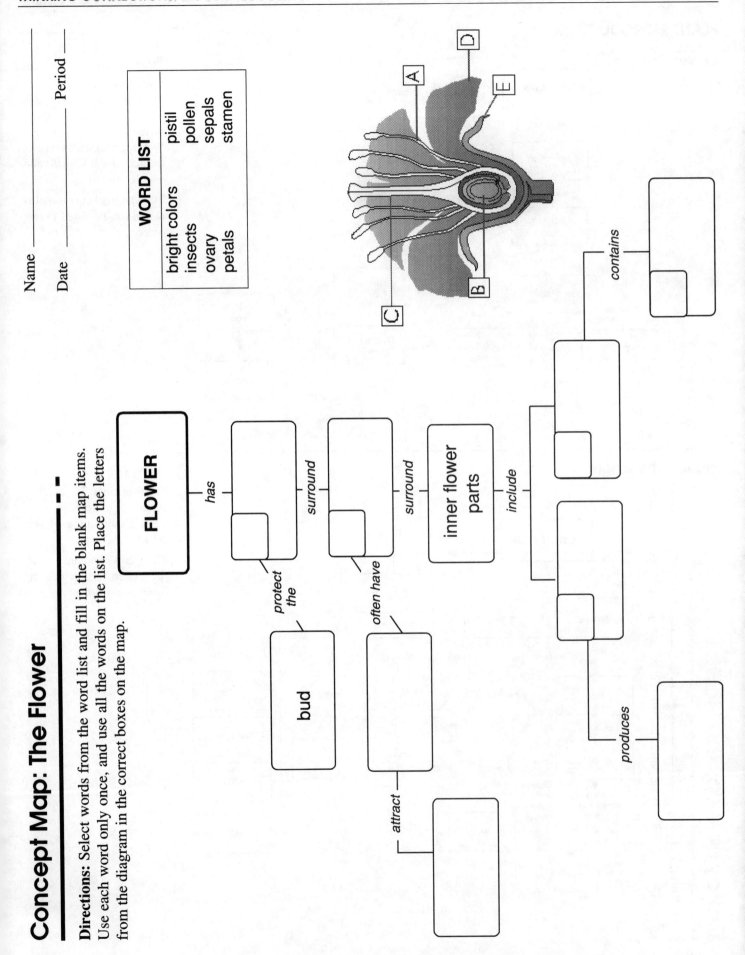

Name _____

Date _____

Period _____

Concept Map: The Flower

Directions: Select words from the word list and fill in the blank map items. Use each word only once, and use all the words on the list. Place the letters from the diagram in the correct boxes on the map.

WORD LIST

bright colors	ovary
bud	petals
embryos	pistil
female sex cells	pollen
fertilized	seeds
inner parts	sepals
insects	stamen
male sex grains	

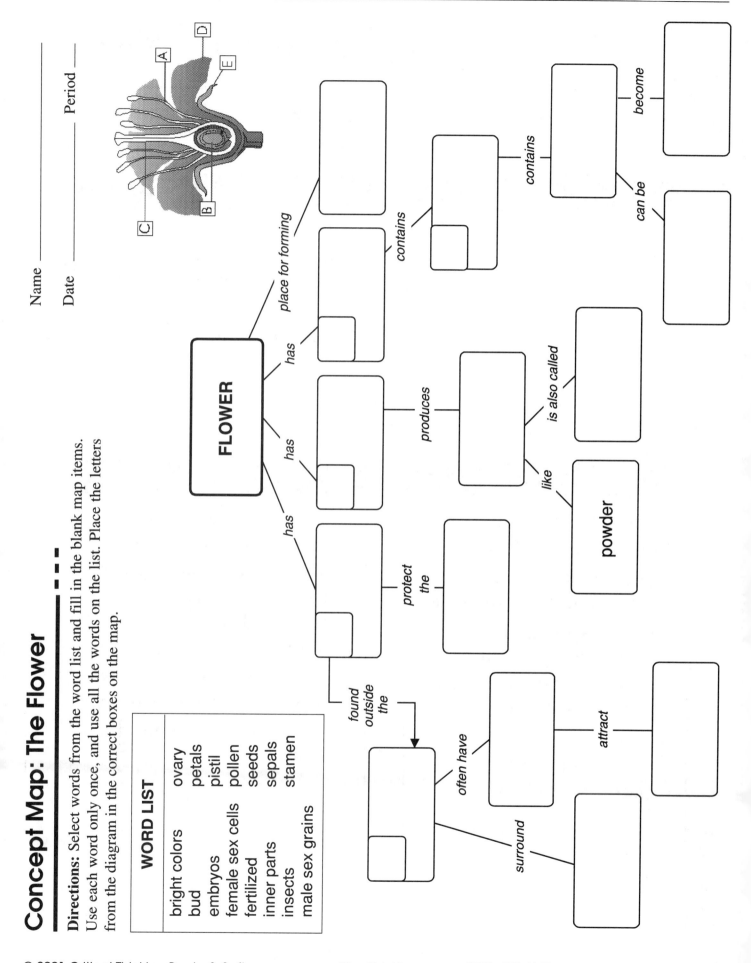

Critical Thinking → C⚲NCEPT FILE

The Flower

Function

For many plants, the flower is the organ of reproduction.

The seeds of the plant form deep in the tissues of the flower.

Vocabulary

- ☐ **female sex cell**—produced in the ovary, this cell becomes the embryo when it is fertilized
- ☐ **male sex grain**—another name for pollen

Flower Parts

There are four main parts to a flower.

- sepals—the outer parts, they protect the flower bud
- petals—just inside the sepals, the petals often have bright colors, which attract insects and other animals
- stamen—produces pollen
- pistil—contains the ovary

Inner Parts

- stamen—there are usually many of these around the pistil in the center. Stamens produce a powder that is called pollen.
- pistil—there is usually one pistil in the center of the flower. It contains the ovary, where the female sex cell forms.

THE FLOWER

Lower Challenge

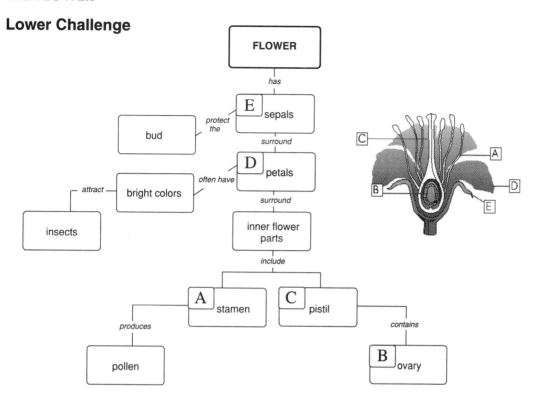

Score: 12 (7 words and 5 letters)

Starting hints: The connector *attract* on the left suggests *insects* below and *bright colors* above.

The flower is layered, so sepals surround petals, which further surround the inner parts.

Diagram Key:

A   stamen
B   ovary
C   pistil
D   petal
E   sepal

Higher Challenge

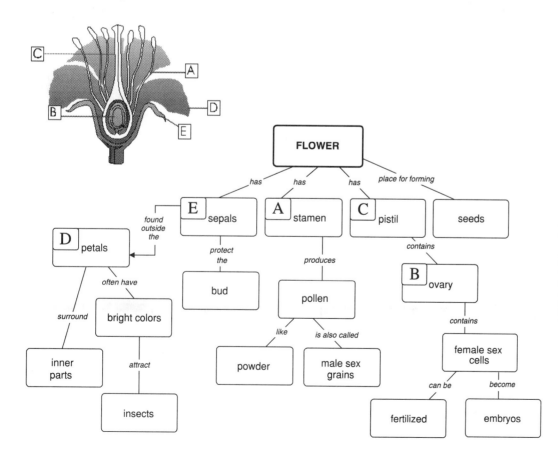

Score: 19 (14 words and 5 letters)

Starting hints: The connector *attract* on the bottom left suggests insects below and bright colors above.

The connector and item on the lower right, *can be fertilized*, points to female sex cells (the male sex grains, or pollen, cannot be fertilized). The item *powder* (lower center) suggests the pollen above.

Diagram Key:

A   stamen
B   ovary
C   pistil
D   petal
E   sepal

Concept Map: Seeds

Name _____

Date _____

Period _____

WORD LIST

apple	one seed
bean	water
cherry	wind
cones	fruits
	conifers
	evergreen
	many seeds

Directions: Select words from the word list and fill in the blank map items. Use each word only once, and use all the words on the list.

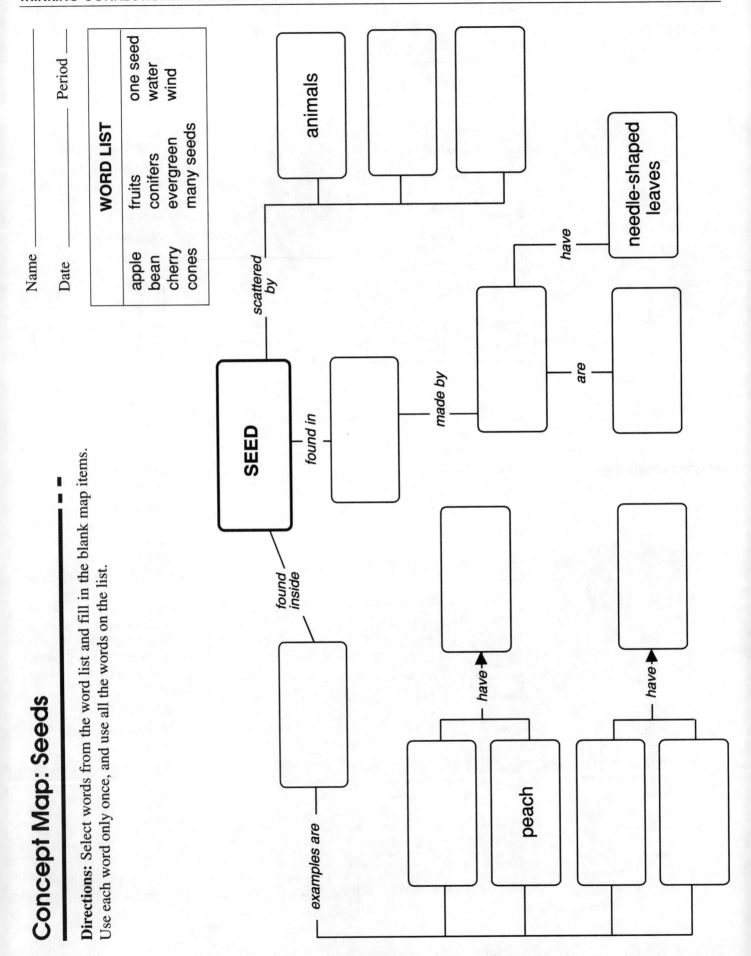

Concept Map: Seeds

Directions: Select words from the word list and fill in the blank map items. Use each word only once, and use all the words on the list.

Name _____

Date _____ Period _____

WORD LIST

animals	conifers
apple	enlarged ovary
bean	evergreen
cherry	flower
cones	fruit
	peach
	water
	wind

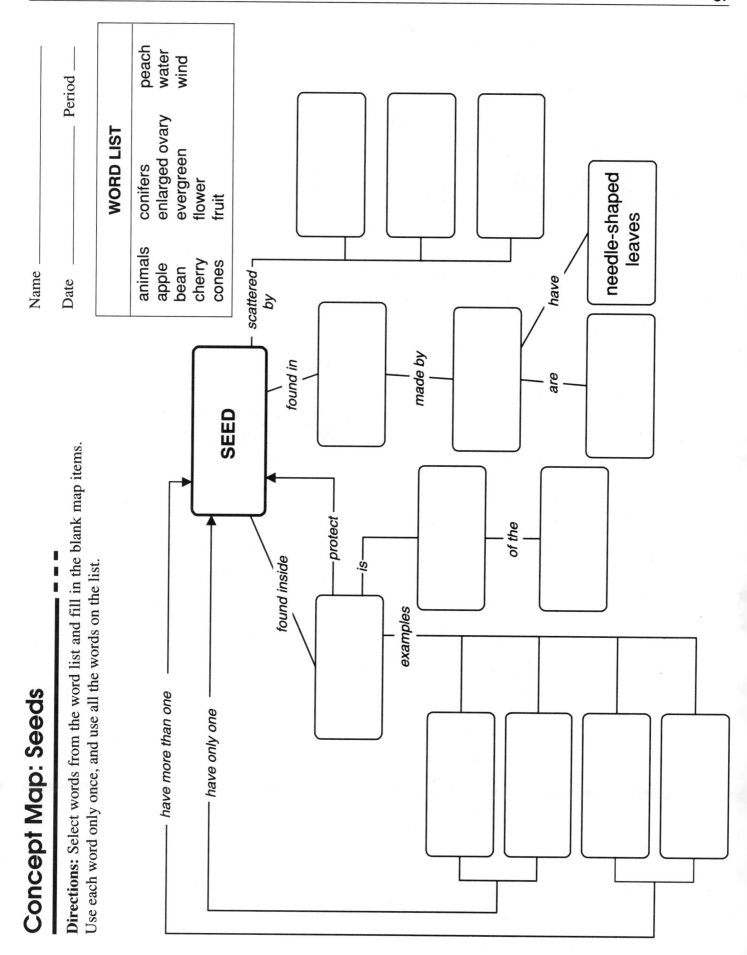

Critical Thinking → C**ONCEPT FILE**

Seeds

Where Are They Formed?

Conifers
- form seeds in cones

Flowers
- form seeds inside the flower

Vocabulary

☐ **conifer**—evergreen plant with needle-shaped leaves

☐ **evergreen**—a plant that does not lose its leaves

☐ **ovary**—the part of the flower that makes the egg

Fruit

The "fruit" of a plant is an enlarged ovary which contains seeds.

- the fruit protects seeds
- two types of fruit
  - some contain many seeds, like apples and beans
  - some contain one seed, like cherries and peaches

SEEDS

Lower Challenge

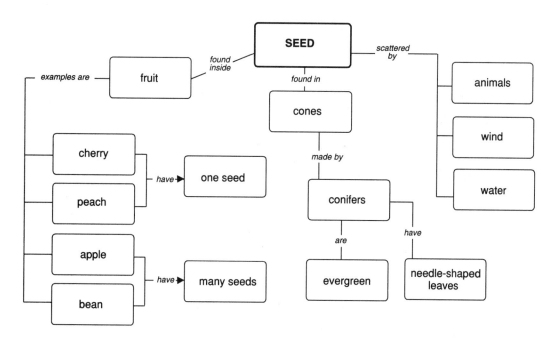

Score: 11 words

Starting hints: The seed item *peach* suggests the items *cherry* and *one seed*.

The item on the lower right, *needle-shaped leaves*, is a characteristic of conifers.

The fruits with *many seeds*, apple and bean, can be listed in either order.

Higher Challenge

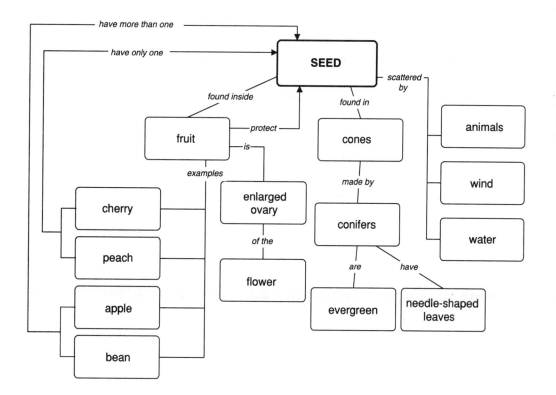

Score: 14 words

Starting hints: The connector *scattered by* is a good start, as it points to animals, wind, and water (in no particular order).

The connectors *have more than one* and *have only one* refer to the number of seeds in fruits.

Name ————————
Date ————————
Period ————————

Concept Map: Photosynthesis

Directions: Select words from the word list and fill in the blank map items.
Use each word only once, and use all the words on the list.

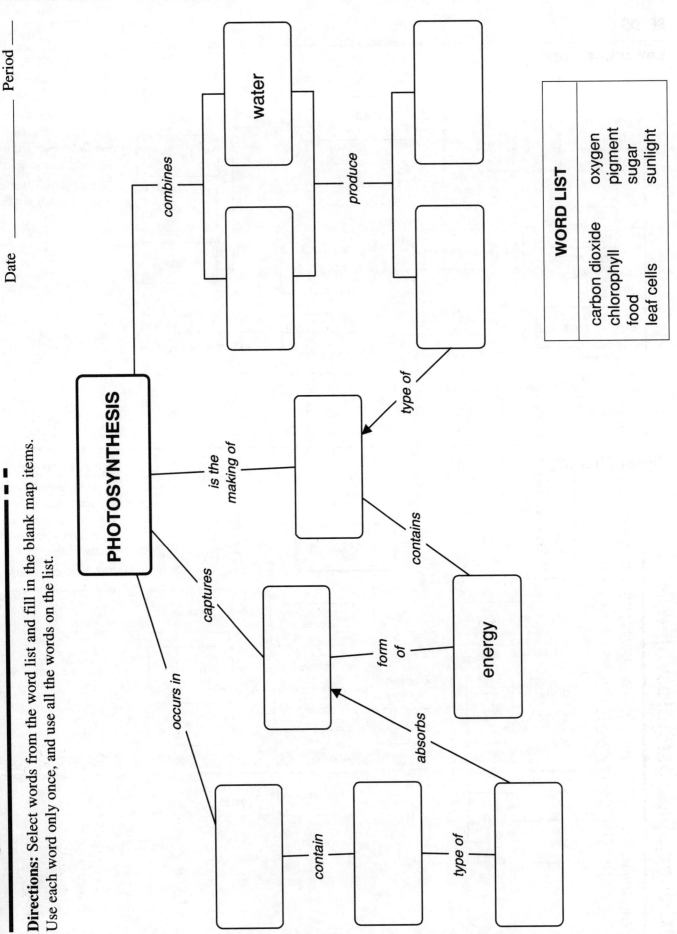

Concept Map: Photosynthesis

Name _____

Date _____

Period _____

Directions: Select words from the word list and fill in the blank map items.
Use each word only once, and use all the words on the list.

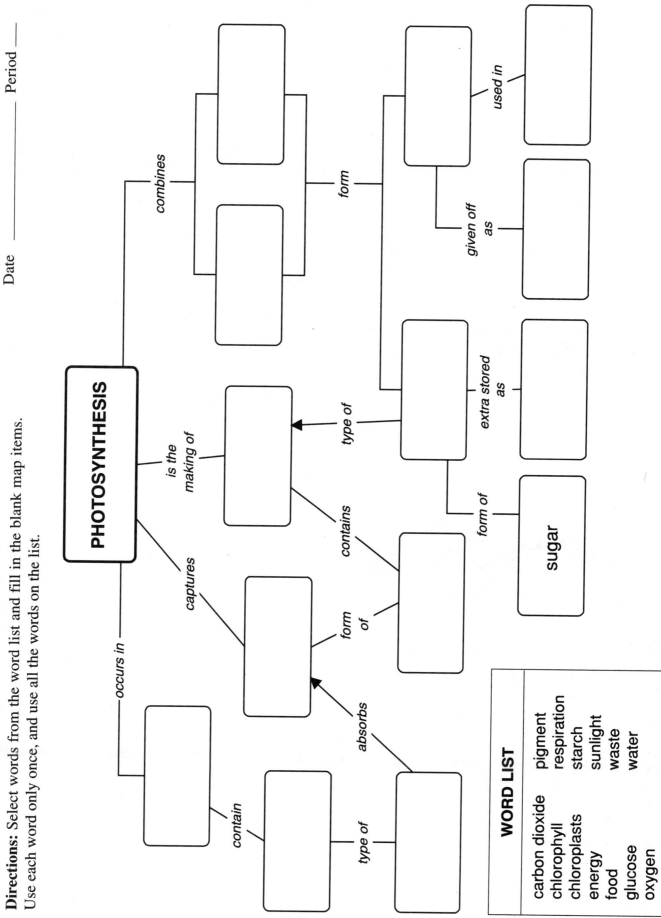

WORD LIST

carbon dioxide	pigment
chlorophyll	respiration
chloroplasts	starch
energy	sunlight
food	waste
glucose	water
oxygen	

Critical Thinking → CONCEPT FILE

Photosynthesis

What It Is

Photosynthesis is the process that plants use to make food. In most plants, photosynthesis takes place in the leaf cells.

What Goes In

The plant uses three things to make food:

- sunlight—a type of energy
- carbon dioxide
- water

What Comes Out

There are two products of photosynthesis:

- glucose—a simple sugar and a form of food. Sugar that the plant doesn't use right away might be stored as starch.
- oxygen—a gas that is given off as a waste product

Vocabulary

- ☐ **chlorophyll**—a green pigment in leaves that performs photosynthesis
- ☐ **chloroplasts**—the parts of the leaf's cells that contain chlorophyll
- ☐ **respiration**—the process of using energy. Plants and animals use oxygen as part of respiration.

PHOTOSYNTHESIS

Lower Challenge

Score: 8 words

Starting hints: The connector *is the making of* points directly to the item *food*. The seed *water* on the right is best paired with carbon dioxide.

The connector *captures* points to *sunlight* below it.

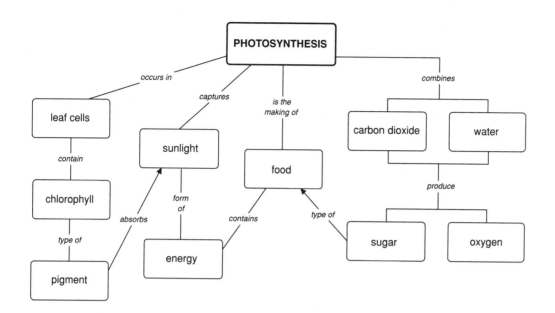

Higher Challenge

Score: 12 words

Starting hints: The connector *is the making of* points directly to the item *food*. The connector *captures* points to *sunlight* below it.

The seed item and connector *form of sugar* points back to glucose.

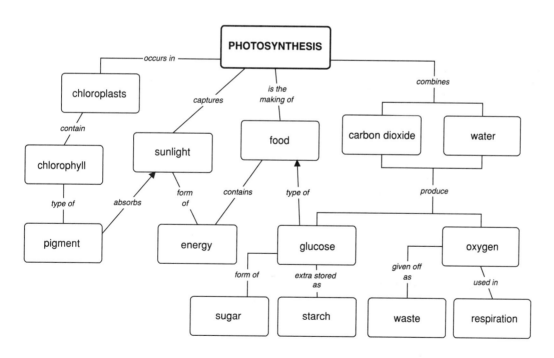

Concept Map: Invertebrates

Name _____

Period _____

Date _____

WORD LIST

arthropods
backbone
jellyfish
jointed legs
mollusks
worms

Directions: Select words from the word list and fill in the blank map items. Use each word only once, and use all the words on the list. Cut out the pictures in the picture gallery and paste or tape them in the correct boxes.

insect

lobster

snail

scallop

spider

clam

INVERTEBRATES

one group is

example is

earthworm

one group is

most have examples

shells

one group is

examples

include

have no

have

Concept Map: Invertebrates

Directions: Select words from the word list and fill in the blank map items. Use each word only once, and use all the words on the list. Cut out the pictures in the picture gallery and paste or tape them in the correct boxes.

Name _____

Date _____

Period _____

WORD LIST

arthropods	mollusks
backbone	pores
cnidarians	sponges
jellyfish	worms
jointed legs	

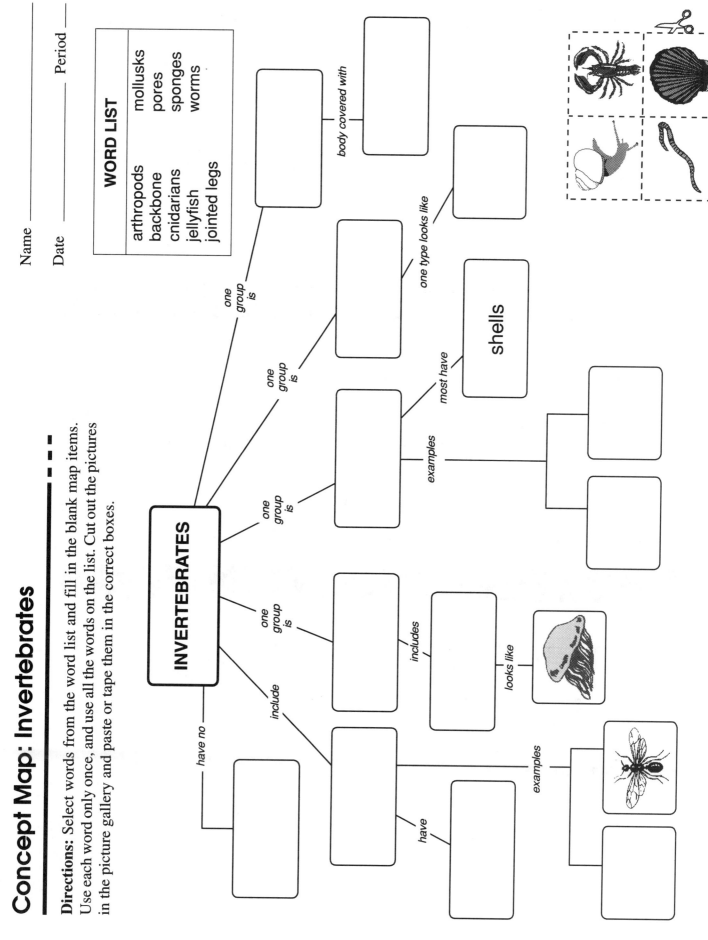

INVERTEBRATES

- *one group is* — *body covered with*
- *one group is* — *one type looks like* — *most have* **shells** — *examples*
- *one group is* — *examples*
- *one group is* — *includes* — *looks like*
- *include* — *examples* — *have*
- *have no*

Critical Thinking →  **C NCEPT FILE**

Invertebrates

Vocabulary

- ❏ **invertebrate**—an animal without a backbone
- ❏ **pore**—a small opening in the skin

Groups

Arthropods

- have jointed legs
- include insects, spiders, lobsters, millipedes

Mollusks

- most have at least one shell
- include clams, snails, scallops

Worms

- include earthworms, bloodworms, leeches

Other Groups

Cnidarians

- include jellyfish, corals, anemones

Sponges

- bodies are covered with pores

INVERTEBRATES

Lower Challenge

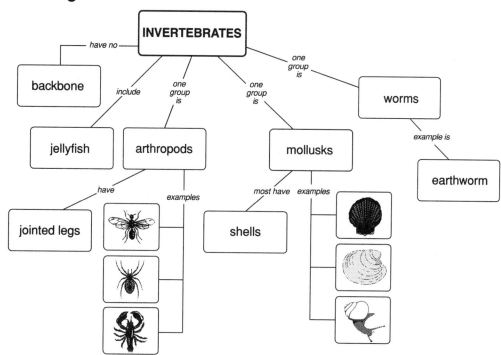

Score: 12 (6 words and 6 pictures)

Starting hints: The seed item *shells* is a clear indication of the *mollusks* group. The pictures of the scallop, clam, and snail can be in any order here.

The only other group with picture examples is the arthropods. Again, the pictures of the insect, lobster and spider can be in any order.

Higher Challenge

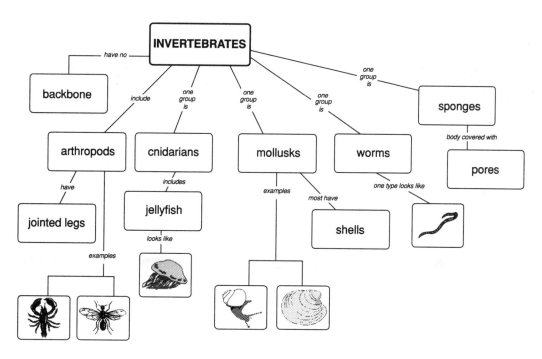

Score: 13 (9 words and 4 pictures)

Starting hints: The seed item *shells* is a clear indication of the *mollusks* group.

The jellyfish picture indicates the item *jellyfish* and, above it, the group cnidarians.

Concept Map: Sponge

Directions: Select words from the word list to fill in the blank map items.
Use each word only once, and use all the words on the list.

Name _____

Date _____

Period _____

WORD LIST

food
pores
ocean
one place
plant
skeleton
water

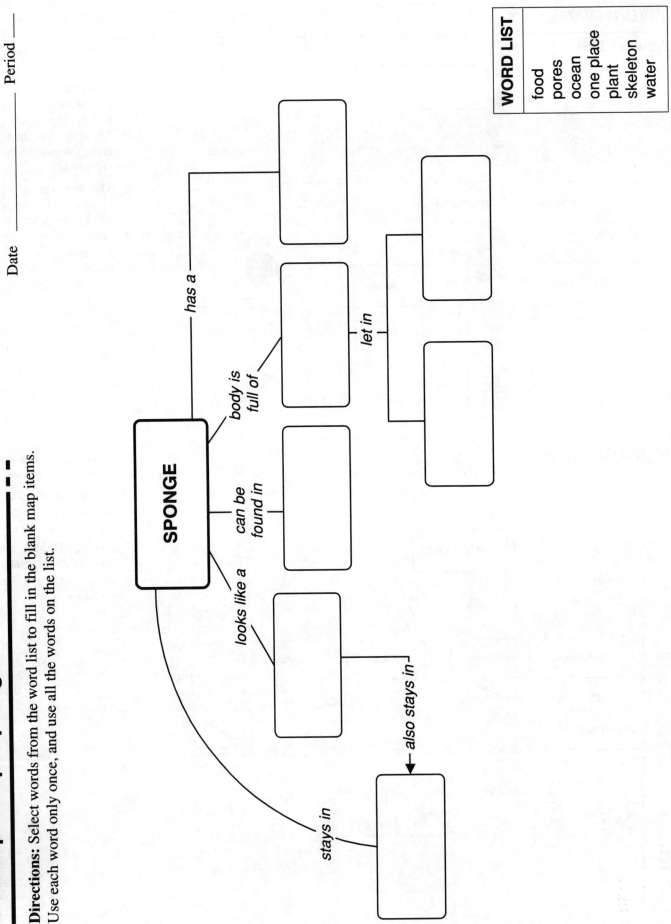

SPONGE

has a

body is full of

can be found in

looks like a

stays in

let in

also stays in

Concept Map: Sponge

Directions: Select words from the word list to fill in the blank map items.
Use each word only once, and use all the words on the list.

Name _____
Date _____
Period _____

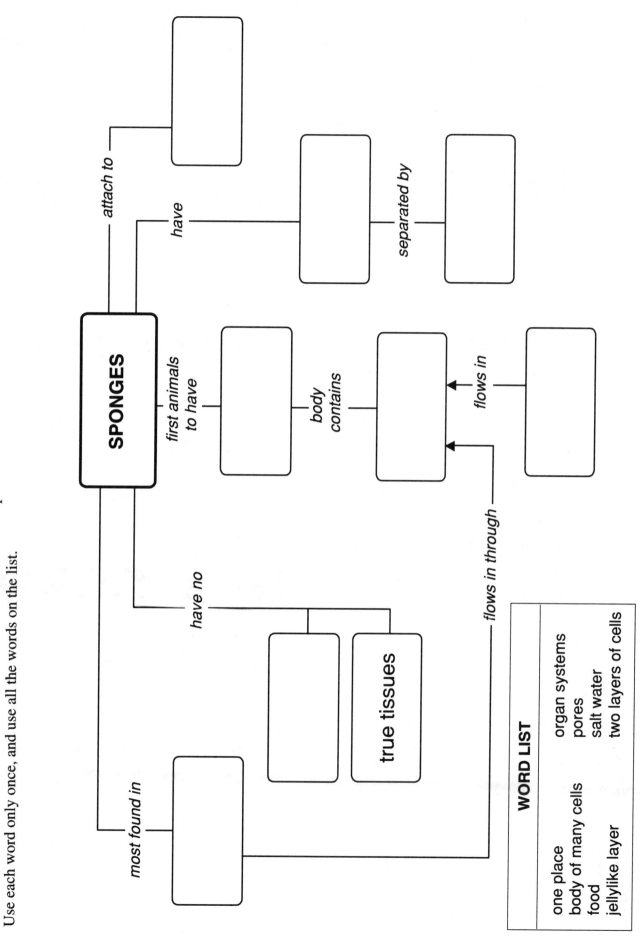

WORD LIST

one place
body of many cells
food
jellylike layer

organ systems
pores
salt water
two layers of cells

Critical Thinking → C NCEPT FILE

Sponges

Structure

The body of the sponge has

- a skeleton that can be hard and spiky or soft and rubbery
- no true tissues
- no organ systems
- many cells (first animals to have)

The cells

- each have a specific job
- are arranged in two layers
- are separated by a jellylike layer

Vocabulary

☐ **pore**—a small hole in the sponge body that lets in water and food

Where they live

Sponges

- live in water—most live in salt water
- do not move around and are attached to one spot

Appearance

The sponge body

- looks like a plant
- has pores
- has canals that carry water
- comes in many shapes, sizes, and colors

SPONGES

Lower Challenge

Score: 7 terms
Starting hints: The connectors *looks like* and *found in* are good starting points.

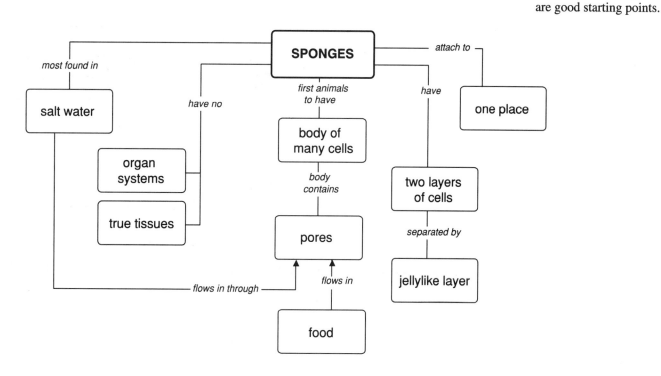

Higher Challenge

Score: 8 words
Starting hints: The connectors *looks like* and *found in* are good starting points.

Concept Map: Cnidarians

Name _____

Date _____

Period _____

Directions: Select words from the word list and fill in the blank map items. Use each word only once, and use all the words on the list. Cut out the pictures in the picture gallery and paste or tape them in the correct boxes.

WORD LIST

coral
hollow body
jellyfish
prey
stinging cells
tentacles
water

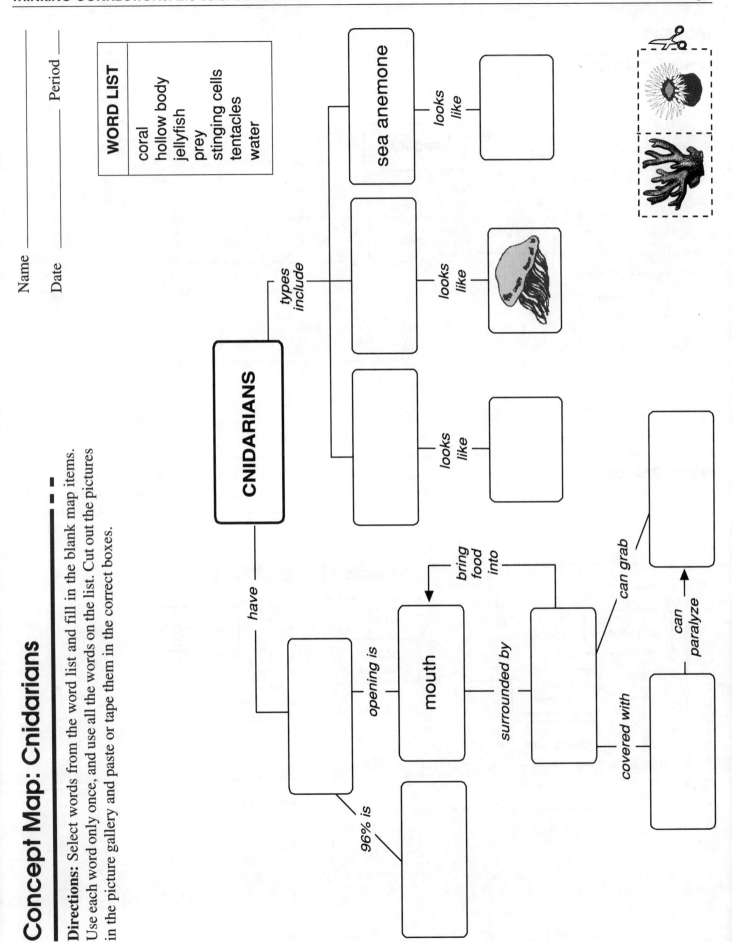

Concept Map: Cnidarians

Directions: Select words from the word list and fill in the blank map items. Use each word only once, and use all the words on the list. Cut out the pictures in the picture gallery and paste or tape them in the correct boxes.

Name ————

Date ————

Period ————

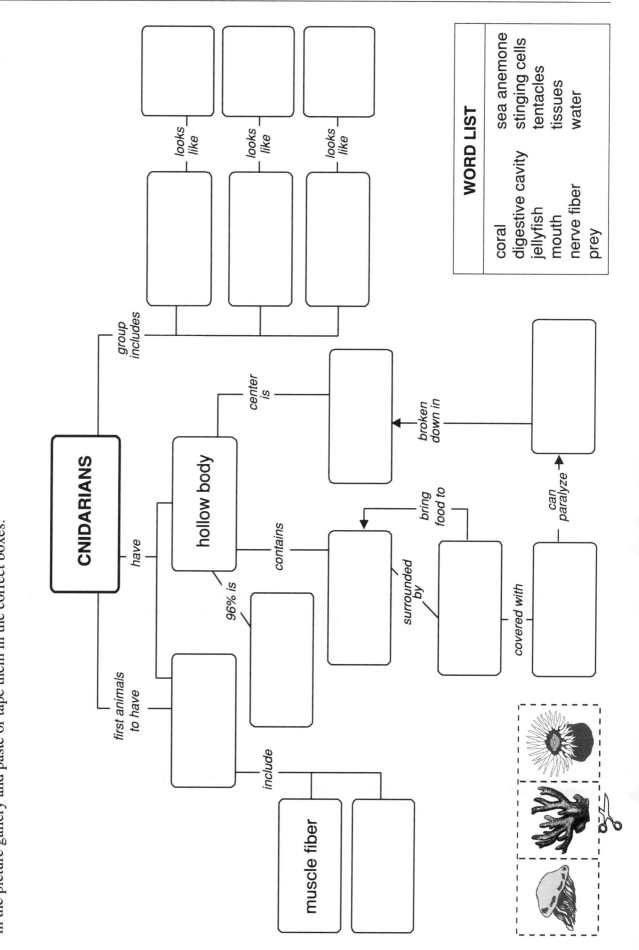

WORD LIST

coral	sea anemone
digestive cavity	stinging cells
jellyfish	tentacles
mouth	tissues
nerve fiber	water
prey	

CNIDARIANS

group includes

looks like (×3)

have

hollow body

first animals to have

center is

contains

96% is

broken down in

bring food to

surrounded by

can paralyze

covered with

include

muscle fiber

Critical Thinking →

Cnidarians

Characteristics

Cnidarians are simple animals with these characteristics:

- hollow body made of 96% water
- a mouth surrounded by tentacles
- first type of animal to have tissues
  - muscle fiber
  - nerve fiber
- has a digestive cavity at the center of the body

Vocabulary

- ❑ **stinging cells**—cells covering the tentacles contain a poison that can paralyze prey
- ❑ **tentacles**—armlike structures that surround the mouth. The tentacles bring food to the mouth.

Types

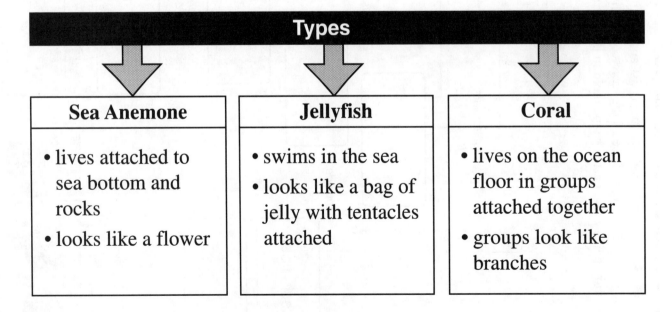

Sea Anemone

- lives attached to sea bottom and rocks
- looks like a flower

Jellyfish

- swims in the sea
- looks like a bag of jelly with tentacles attached

Coral

- lives on the ocean floor in groups attached together
- groups look like branches

CNIDARIANS

Lower Challenge

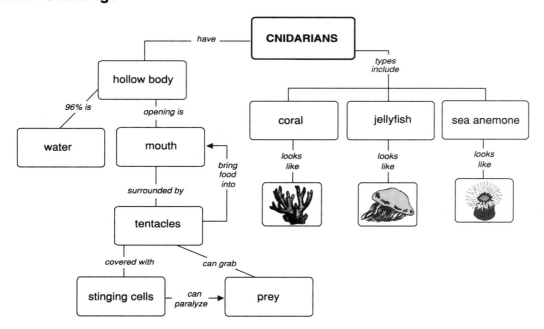

Score: 9 (7 words and 2 pictures)

Starting hints: The seed item *mouth* and the connectors *surrounded by* and *bring food to* both suggest the item *tentacles* below.

The item *sea anemone* on the right is a good place to start matching pictures to items.

Higher Challenge

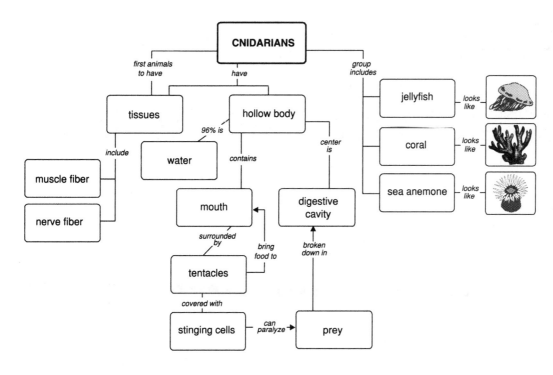

Score: 14 (11 words and 3 pictures)

Starting hints: The connectors *surrounded by* and *bring food to* point to the item *mouth*.

The three groups on the right can be listed in any order, but each picture must match its correct label.

Concept Map: Jellyfish

Name _____

Date _____

Period _____

Directions: Select words from the word list to fill in the blank map items.
Use each word only once, and use all the words on the list.

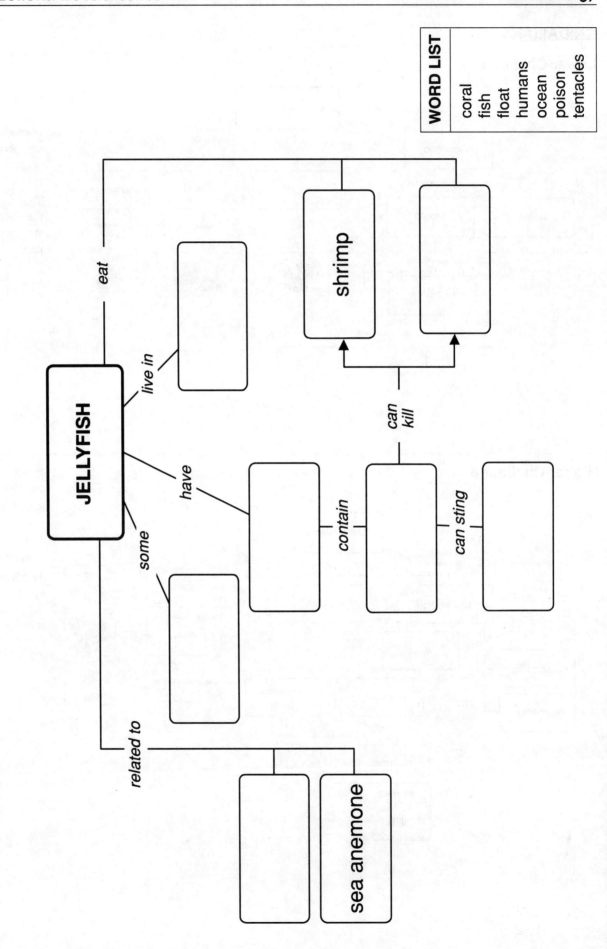

Concept Map: Jellyfish

Name _____

Date _____

Period _____

Directions: Select words from the word list to fill in the blank map items.
Use each word only once, and use all the words on the list.

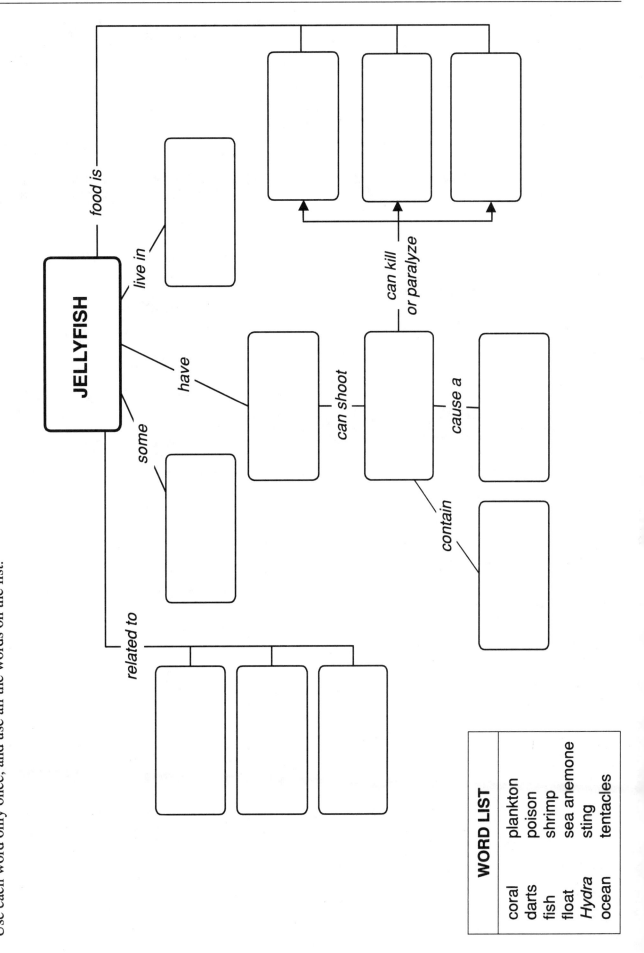

WORD LIST

coral	plankton
darts	poison
fish	shrimp
float	sea anemone
Hydra	sting
ocean	tentacles

Critical Thinking ➡️ C💡NCEPT FILE

Jellyfish

Where It Lives

- Most live in the ocean.
- Many eat shrimp or fish.
- Others eat plankton.

Characteristics

Although they can swim, many will simply float from place to place.

- have tentacles
  - have tiny darts that contain poison
  - darts can sting and will kill or paralyze the food the jellyfish eats
- related to
  - sea anemone
  - coral
  - *Hydra*

Vocabulary

☐ **plankton**—tiny plants and animals that drift on the ocean surface

JELLYFISH

Lower Challenge

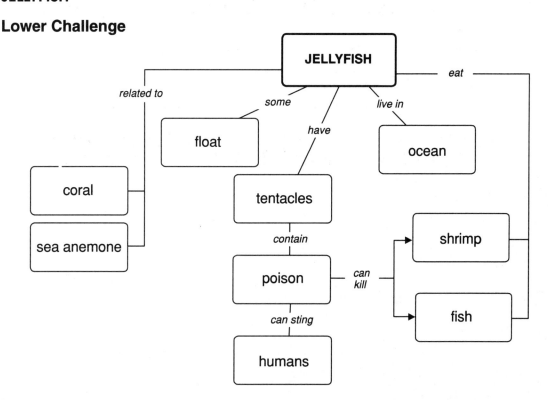

Score: 7 words

Starting hints: At the bottom left is the item *sea anemone* and the connector *related to* above it. The right choice is *coral* in the block above.

The connector *eat* leads to *shrimp*. The other food choice is *fish*.

Higher Challenge

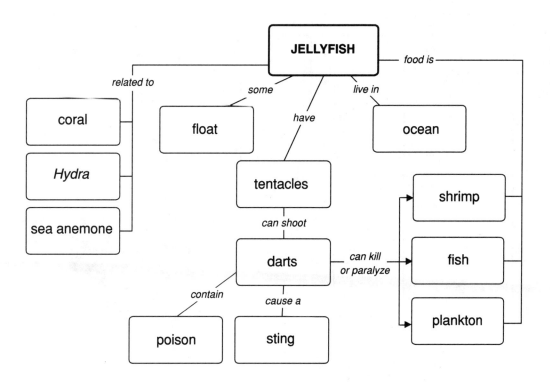

Score: 12 words

Starting hints: The connector *live in* suggests the item *ocean*. The connector *can shoot* suggests *darts*.

The relatives on the left side can be listed in any order.

Concept Map: Corals

Name _____

Date _____

Period _____

Directions: Select words from the word list to fill in the blank map items.
Use each word only once, and use all the words on the list.

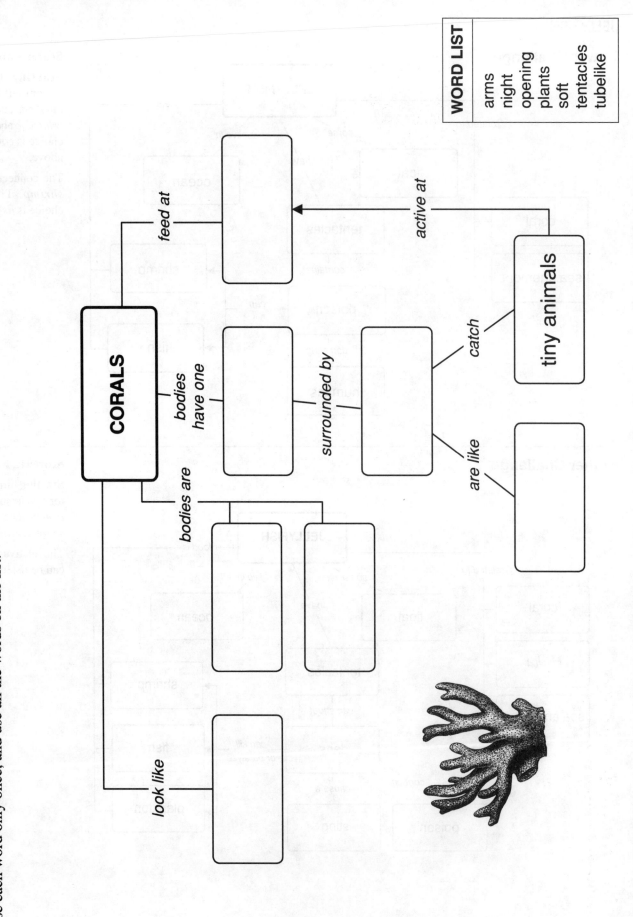

Name _____

Date _____   Period _____

Concept Map: Corals

Directions: Select words from the word list to fill in the blank map items.
Use each word only once, and use all the words on the list.

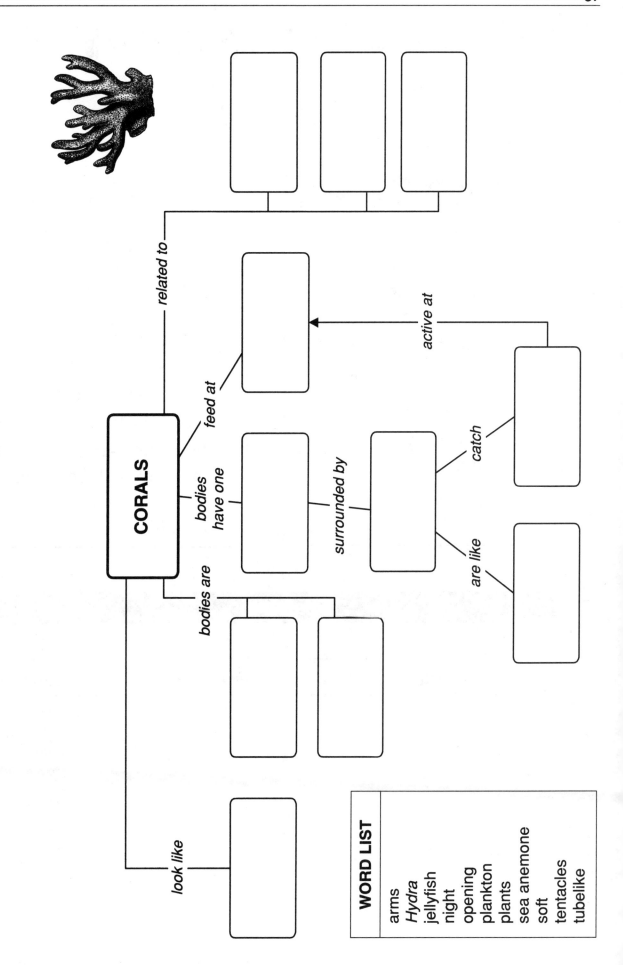

CORALS

related to

feed at

active at

bodies have one

surrounded by

catch

are like

bodies are

look like

WORD LIST
arms
Hydra
jellyfish
night
opening
plankton
plants
sea anemone
soft
tentacles
tubelike

Critical Thinking → C NCEPT FILE

Corals

Characteristics	Vocabulary
• corals have soft, tubelike bodies	❑ **nocturnal**—active only at night
• form mineral skeletons. Many look like plants growing on the ocean floor.	❑ **plankton**—tiny plants and animals that drift on the surface of the ocean
• body has one opening	❑ **stinging cells**—cells covering the tentacles. Contain a poison that can paralyze prey.
• opening is surrounded by tentacles that can trap plankton	❑ **tentacles**—armlike structures that surround the mouth. The tentacles can bring food to the mouth.
• are nocturnal	

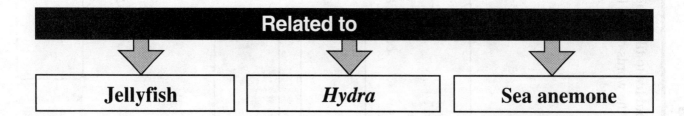

Related to

Jellyfish	*Hydra*	Sea anemone

CORALS

Lower Challenge

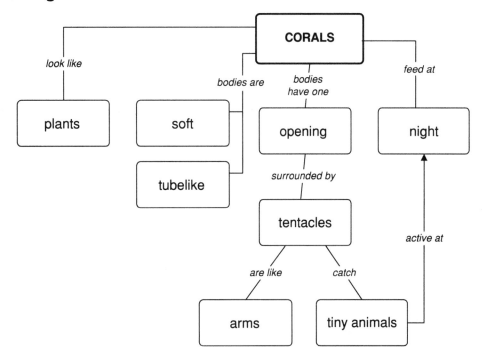

Score: 7 words

Starting hints: The item *opening* best fits under the connector *bodies have one.*

The connector *active at* suggests *night.*

Higher Challenge

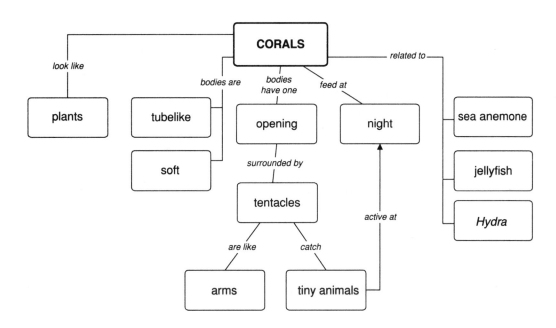

Score: 11 words

Starting hints: The items under the connector *bodies are* can appear in any order, as can the items under the connector *related to.*

Concept Map: Sea Anemones

Directions: Select words from the word list to fill in the blank map items.
Use each word only once, and use all the words on the list.

Name _____

Date _____

Period _____

WORD LIST

coral
food
gliding
Hydra
ocean floor
tentacles
tumbling

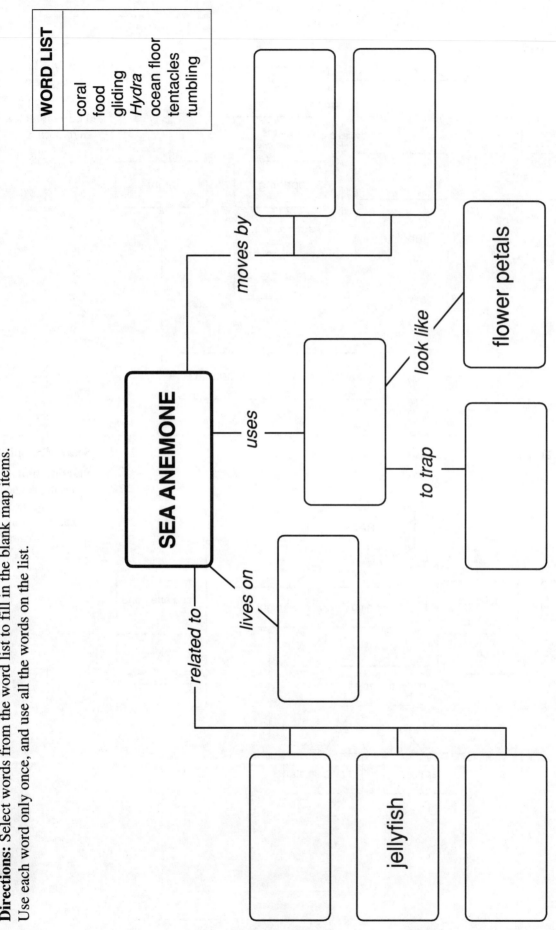

Concept Map: Sea Anemones

Directions: Select words from the word list to fill in the blank map items.
Use each word only once, and use all the words on the list.

Name _____

Date _____

Period _____

WORD LIST	
coral	jellyfish
flower petals	move
food	ocean floor
Hydra	tentacles
gliding	tumbling

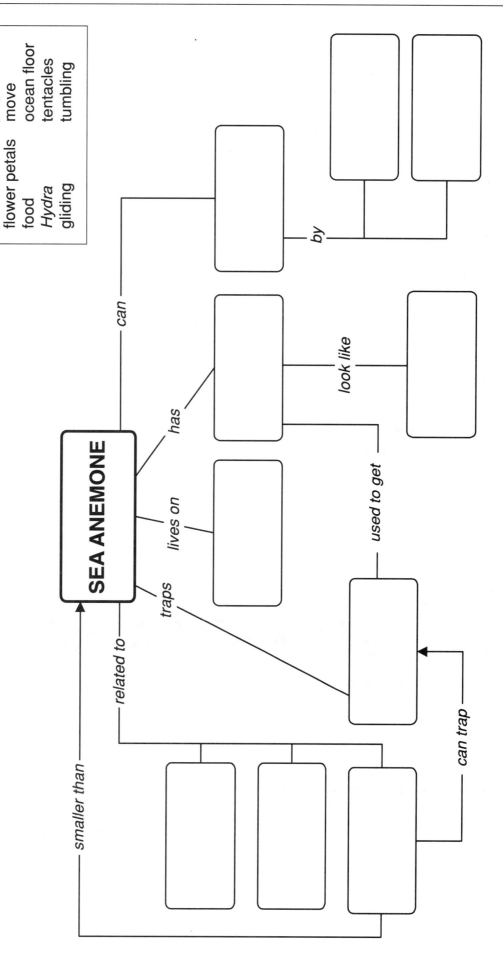

Critical Thinking → C💡NCEPT FILE

Sea Anemone

Feeding

- The sea anemone eats small animals in the water.
- The anemone uses tentacles to trap the animals.
- Tentacles look like flower petals.

Vocabulary

- ❑ **coral**—a tiny relative of the anemone. It lives in large groups and leaves behind stony skeletons.
- ❑ *Hydra*—a small relative of the anemone that lives in fresh water
- ❑ **jellyfish**—larger relatives of the anemone. Many can swim through the water.

Methods of Movement

The sea anemone lives on the ocean floor. It moves by

- gliding
- tumbling

Related to

The sea anemone is related to:
- *Hydra* (much smaller than the anemone)
- coral (also lives attached to ocean floor)
- jellyfish

SEA ANEMONE

Lower Challenge

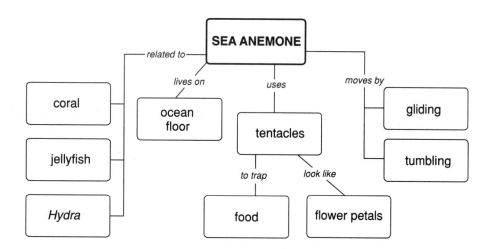

Score: 7 words

Starting hints: The combination of *look like* and *flower petals* points to *tentacles*.

Higher Challenge

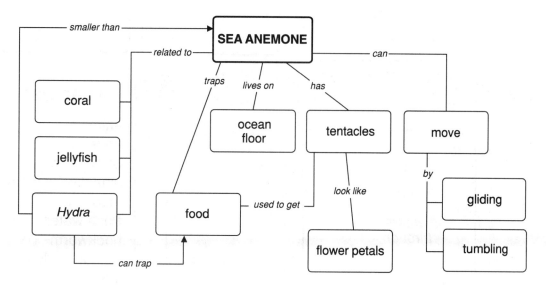

Score: 10 words

Starting hints: The anemone is related to the three types of animals listed, but the *Hydra* traps food in a similar way.

The items *gliding* and *tumbling* in the list are together in the map.

The item *flower petals*, bottom, is not an animal structure but matches the *look like* connector.

Concept Map: Roundworms

Name _____

Date _____ Period ____

Directions: Select words from the word list to fill in the blank map items. Use each word only once, and use all the words on the list.

ROUNDWORMS

have tubelike

most are

some are

have

has two

called

called

free-living

live in

mouth

for

for

example is

live in

plants

enters through

lives in

of

skin

of →

WORD LIST

animals
anus
body
digestive system
food
fresh water
hookworm
human body
intestine
openings
parasites
salt water
soil
wastes

Concept Map: Roundworms

Name _____

Date _____ Period _____

Directions: Select words from the word list to fill in the blank map items. Use each word only once, and use all the words on the list.

WORD LIST

animals	openings
anus	organ systems
digestive	parasites
free-living	salt water
fresh water	skin
hookworm	*Trichina* worm
human intestine	tubelike body
nervous system	

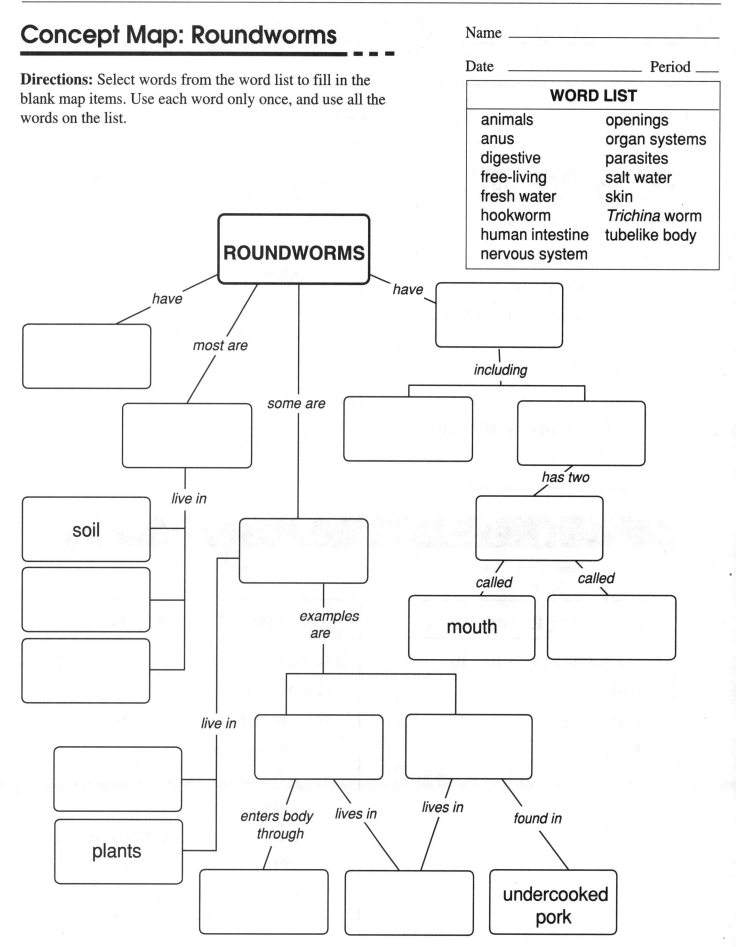

Critical Thinking →  C⚡NCEPT FILE

Roundworms

Body Parts

The body is the shape of a tube.
The body has organ systems.

- nervous system
- digestive system has two openings
  - mouth: where food goes in
  - anus: where wastes come out

Vocabulary

- ❏ **free-living**—an organism that is not attached or inside another living thing
- ❏ **parasite**—an organism that lives on or in another living thing

Types

Free-living Roundworms

These roundworms live in
- soil
- salt water
- fresh water

Parasite Roundworms

Examples are:
- Hookworm
  - enters the human body through the skin
  - lives in intestine
- *Trichina* worm
  - comes from undercooked pork
  - lives in human intestine

ROUNDWORMS

Lower Challenge

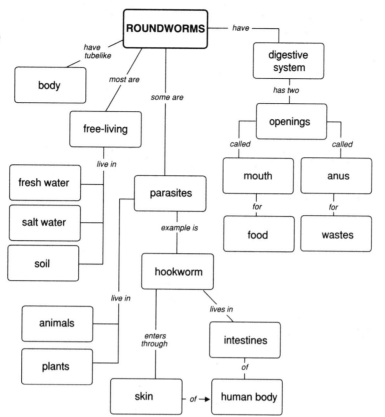

Score: 14 words

Starting hints: Start on the right side at the item *mouth*. The connector below it suggests *food*, and the connector above it suggests the item *openings*.

The connector on the upper left, *have tubelike*, points to the item *body*.

The habitats for roundworms—soil, fresh water, and salt water—can be listed in any order.

Higher Challenge

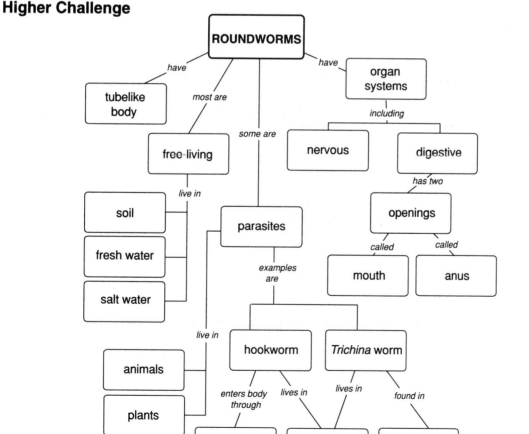

Score: 15 words

Starting hints: On the lower left is the item *plants* with the connector *live in*. This points to the item *parasites*.

The two parasites listed are *Trichina* worm and hookworm; the former is found in undercooked pork.

The habitats for roundworms—soil, fresh water, and salt water—can be listed in any order.

Concept Map: Segmented Worms

Name _____

Date _____ Period ___

Directions: Select words from the word list to fill in the blank map items. Use each word only once, and use all the words on the list.

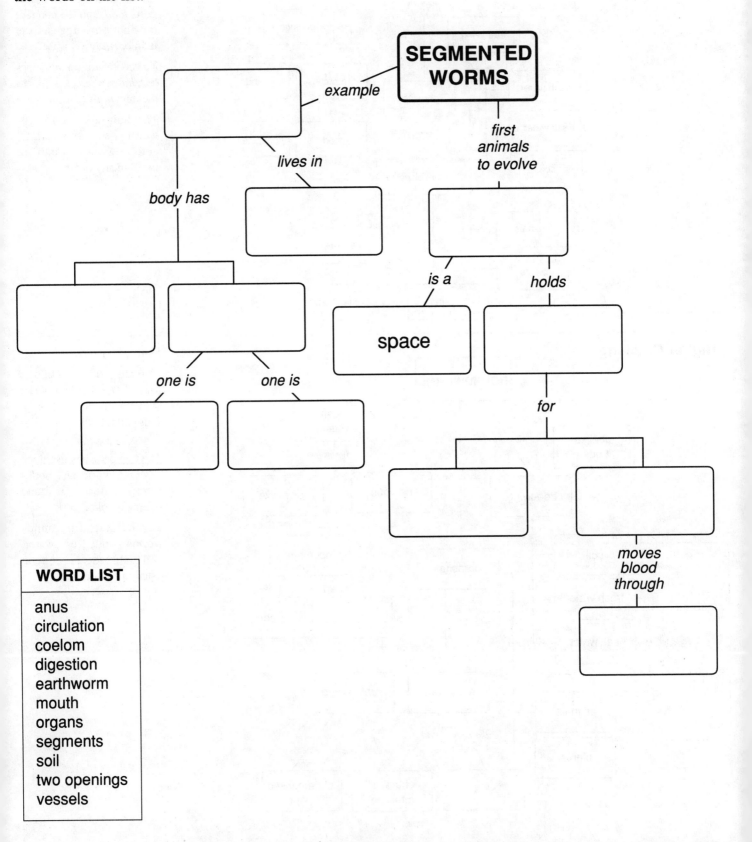

WORD LIST

anus
circulation
coelom
digestion
earthworm
mouth
organs
segments
soil
two openings
vessels

Concept Map: Segmented Worms

Name _____

Date _____ Period _____

Directions: Select words from the word list to fill in the blank map items. Use each word only once, and use all the words on the list.

WORD LIST

anus
circulatory system
coelom
crawling
digestive system
earthworm
fluid
food
mouth
organs
soil
two openings
vessels
wastes

SEGMENTED WORMS

example

first animals to evolve

moves by

body has

lives in

is a

space

holds

filled with

one is

one is

includes

takes in

passes out

moves blood through

Critical Thinking →

Segmented Worms

Characteristics

- body is divided into segments
- body has two openings
  - mouth, which takes in food
  - anus, which passes out wastes
- first animals to develop a coelom
- coelom holds internal organs, including the digestive system and the circulatory system, which moves blood through vessels

Vocabulary

☐ **coelom**—a space or tube inside the body, usually filled with fluid

The Earthworm

- lives in the soil
- moves around by crawling

SEGMENTED WORMS

Lower Challenge

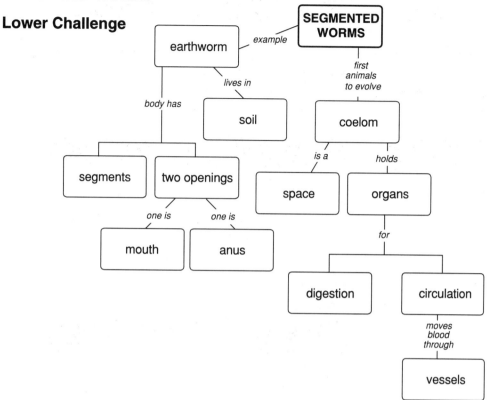

Score: 11 words

Starting hints: The seed item, *space*, defines the coelom.

The connector *moves blood through*, on the lower right, points to the items *vessels* below it and *circulatory system* in the box above.

Higher Challenge

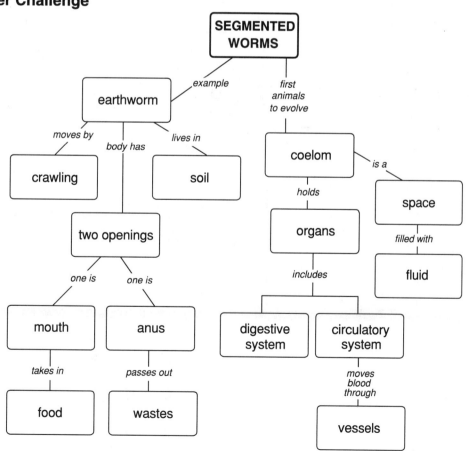

Score: 14 words

Starting hints: See notes above.

The two items *mouth* and *anus* on the lower left are not interchangeable.

Concept Map: Flatworms

Directions: Select words from the word list to fill in the blank map items.
Use each word only once, and use all the words on the list.

Name _____

Date _____

Period _____

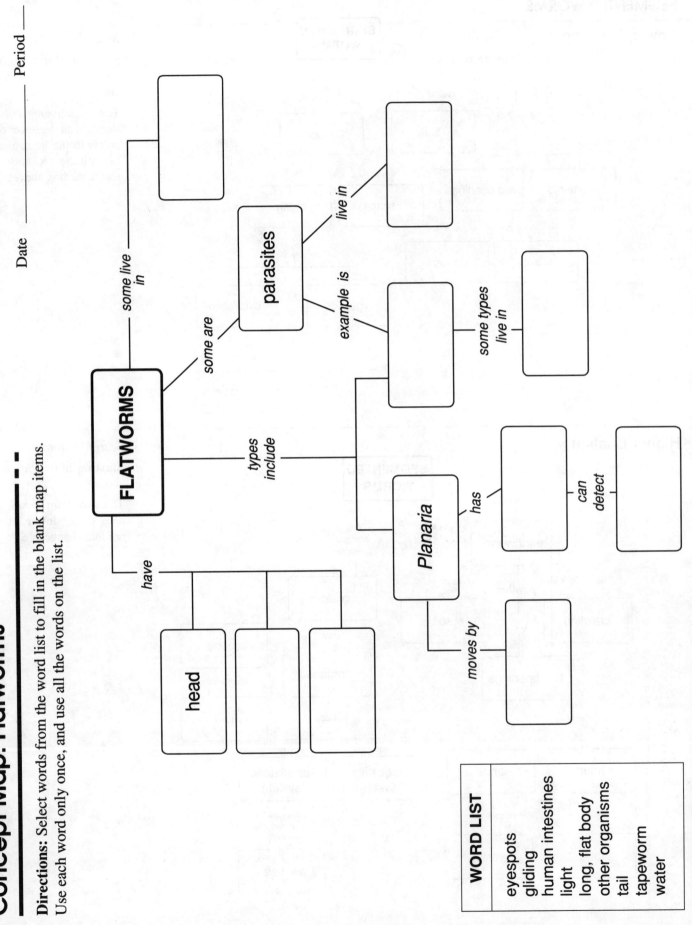

some live in

parasites

live in

some are

FLATWORMS

example is

some types live in

types include

has

can detect

Planaria

have

head

moves by

WORD LIST
eyespots
gliding
human intestines
light
long, flat body
other organisms
tail
tapeworm
water

Concept Map: Flatworms

Directions: Select words from the word list to fill in the blank map items.
Use each word only once, and use all the words on the list.

Name ——————
Date —————— Period ——————

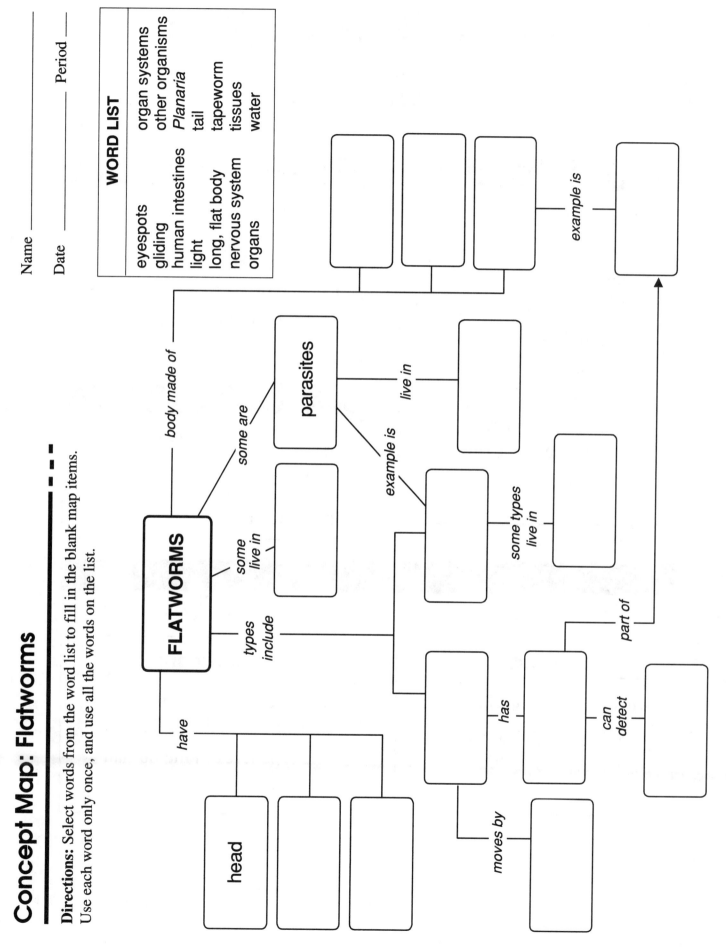

WORD LIST

eyespots	organ systems
gliding	other organisms
human intestines	*Planaria*
light	tail
long, flat body	tapeworm
nervous system	tissues
organs	water

Critical Thinking → C NCEPT FILE

Flatworms

Characteristics

Flatworms have

- a head
- a tail
- a long, flat body made of
  - tissues
  - organs
  - organ systems, which include the nervous system and the digestive system

Vocabulary

❏ **eyespot**—a place on some flatworms (such as *Planaria*) that can detect light

❏ **parasite**—a living thing that lives in or on another living thing

Where They Live

- some (such as *Planaria*) live in the water
- some (such as the tapeworm) are parasites

Types

Planaria

- gets around by gliding
- has two eyespots (as part of its nervous system)

Tapeworm

- a parasite that lives in the intestines of other animals
- one type lives in the human intestine

FLATWORMS

Lower Challenge

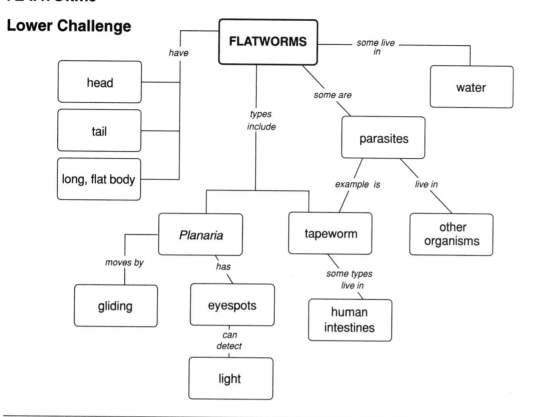

Score: 9 words

Starting hints: Under the connector *types include*, one example, *Planaria*, is given. The other must be *tapeworm*.

On the far right, the combination of connector and item *parasites live in* defines *other organisms*.

Higher Challenge

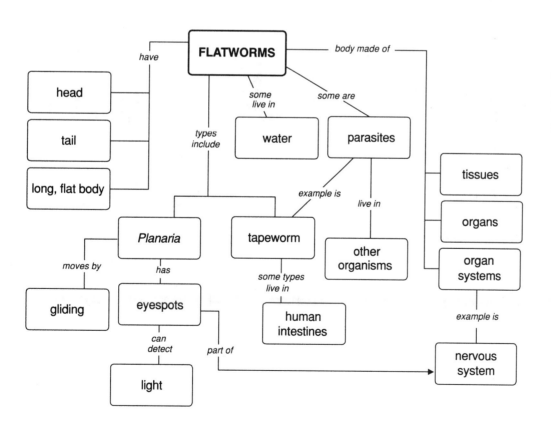

Score: 15 words

Starting hints: On the far right, the item-connector combination *parasites live in* defines *other organisms*.

The seed item *head* suggests the other body descriptions, which can be listed in either order.

Concept Map: Mollusks

Name _____

Date _____   Period _____

Directions: Select words from the word list and fill in the blank map items. Use each word only once, and use all the words on the list. Cut out the pictures in the picture gallery and paste or tape them in the correct boxes.

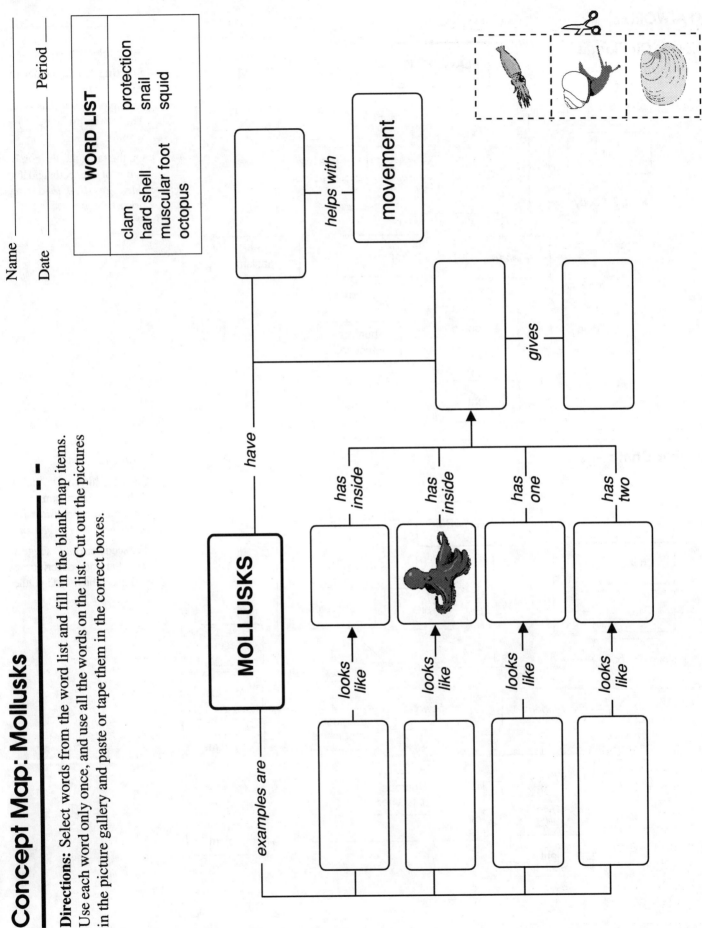

helps with

movement

gives

have

MOLLUSKS

has inside

has inside

has one

has two

looks like

looks like

looks like

looks like

examples are

Concept Map: Mollusks

Directions: Select words from the word list and fill in the blank map items. Use each word only once, and use all the words on the list.

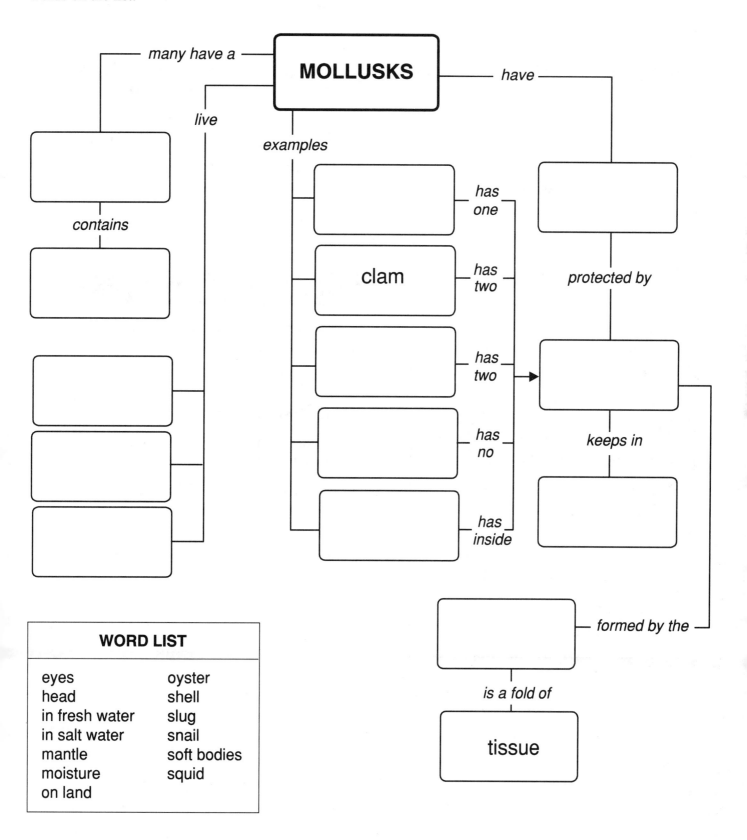

WORD LIST	
eyes	oyster
head	shell
in fresh water	slug
in salt water	snail
mantle	soft bodies
moisture	squid
on land	

 **C NCEPT FILE**

Mollusks

Features

- All have soft bodies.
- Some have a head with eyes.
- Most have hard shells.

The Shell

The mollusk's hard shell protects its soft body and helps to keep moisture inside.

Though a few mollusks have no shell, most have 1 or 2 shells.

- no shell: slug
- one shell (outer): snail
- one shell (inner): squid, octopus
- two shells: clam, oyster

Vocabulary

- ❒ **mantle**—a fold of tissue that forms the shell of a mollusk's soft body.
- ❒ **foot**—a muscular part that helps the animal move around

Where They Live

Mollusks live all over the world. They can be found

- on land
- in fresh water
- in salt water

MOLLUSKS

Lower Challenge

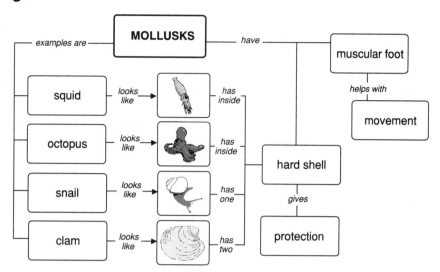

Score: 10 (7 words and 3 pictures)

Starting hints: Start with the picture of the octopus; that will suggest the item *octopus*, which will lead to the item *hard shell*. Also, the connectors *has one* and *has two* will lead to the snail and the clam.

Higher Challenge

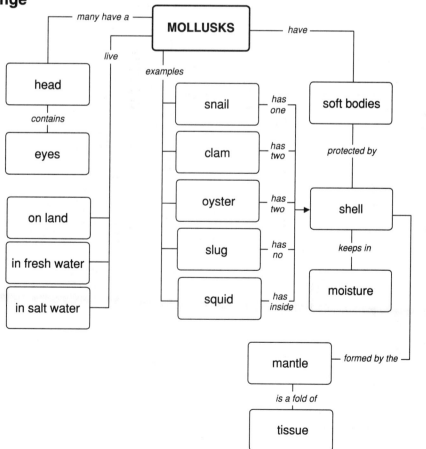

Score: 13 words

Starting hints: The connectors *has one*, *has two*, *has no*, and *has inside* all point to the item *shell*.

The items under the connector *live* are interchangeable.

Concept Map: Arthropods

Name ——————

Date ——————

Period ——————

Directions: Select words from the word list to fill in the blank map items.
Use each word only once, and use all the words on the list.

WORD LIST

insect
on land
legs
outer skeleton
segmented body
spider

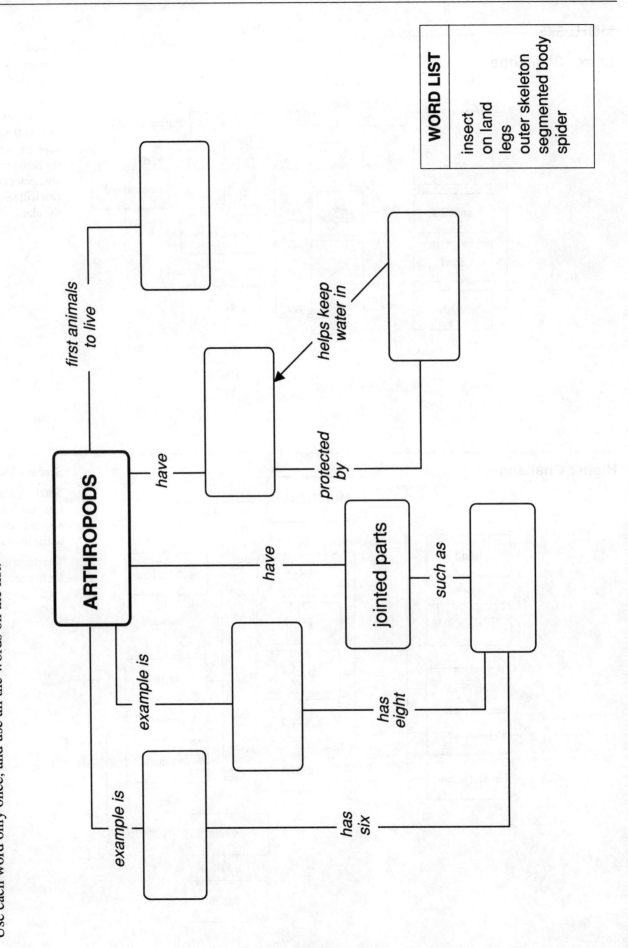

Concept Map: Arthropods - - -

Name _____

Date _____ Period ____

Directions: Select words from the word list to fill in the blank map items. Use each word only once, and use all the words on the list.

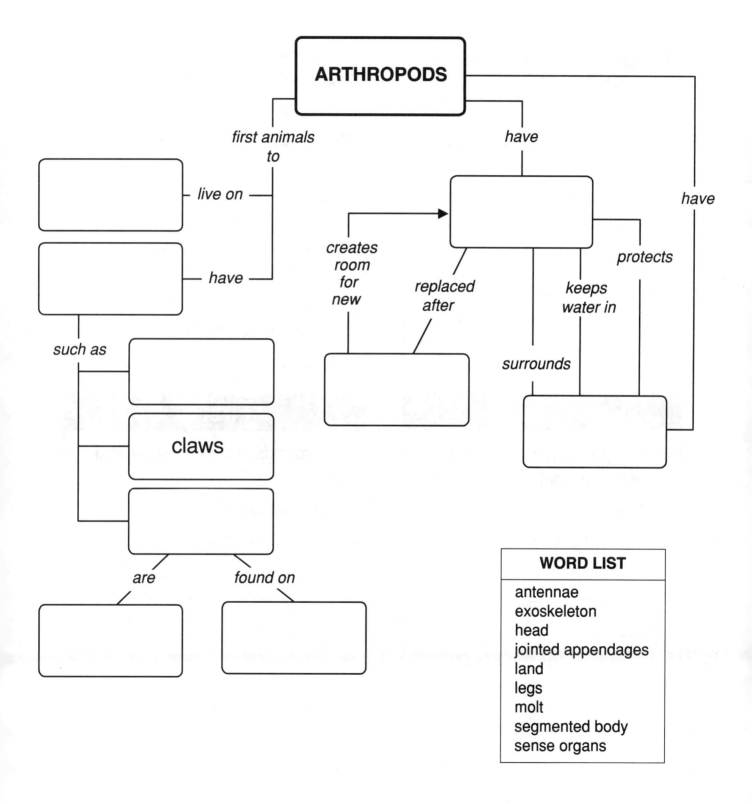

WORD LIST

antennae
exoskeleton
head
jointed appendages
land
legs
molt
segmented body
sense organs

Critical Thinking → C💡NCEPT FILE

Arthropods

Body

- has an exoskeleton
- is sometimes segmented into three parts:
  - head
  - thorax
  - abdomen
- grows during molting
- has jointed appendages

Vocabulary

- ❏ **antennae**—sense organs
- ❏ **exoskeleton**—an outer skeleton that protects the animal and keeps water inside the body
- ❏ **molt**—the shedding of the exoskeleton
- ❏ **thorax**—the middle segment of an insect body

Appendages

Arthropod appendages are jointed and include:

- legs
  - 6 on insects
  - 8 on spiders
  - 10 on crabs
- claws
- antennae (on the head)

Firsts!

Arthropods are the first animals to:

- live on land
- have jointed appendages

ARTHROPODS

Lower Challenge

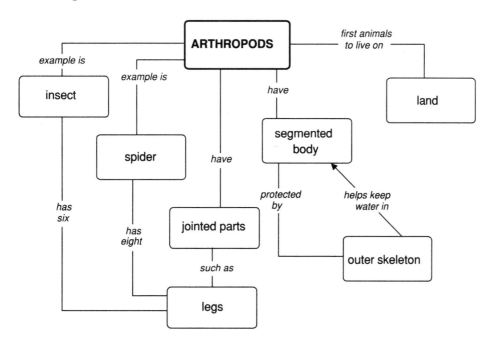

Score: 6 words

Starting hints: This simple map stresses only the characteristics of segmented body and jointed parts. It includes two examples. The connectors *has six* and *has eight* refer to the number of insect and spider legs. The connector *protected by* points to *outer skeleton*.

Higher Challenge

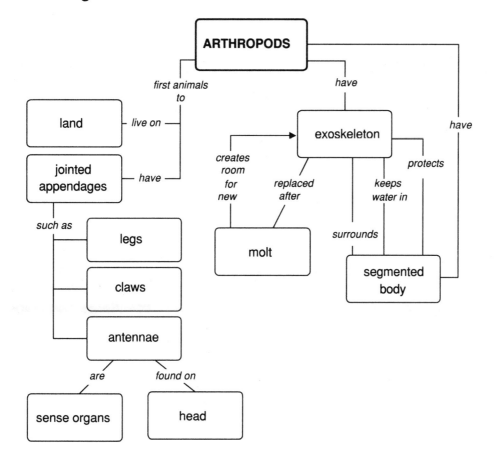

Score: 9 words

Starting hints: The item *claws* is an example of a jointed appendage. The other two, legs and antennae, should fall into place as other examples, with the items at the bottom left restricting the item above them to *antennae*.

Concept Map: Sea Star (Starfish)

Directions: Select words from the word list to fill in the blank map items. Use each word only once, and use all the words on the list.

Name _____

Date _____

Period _____

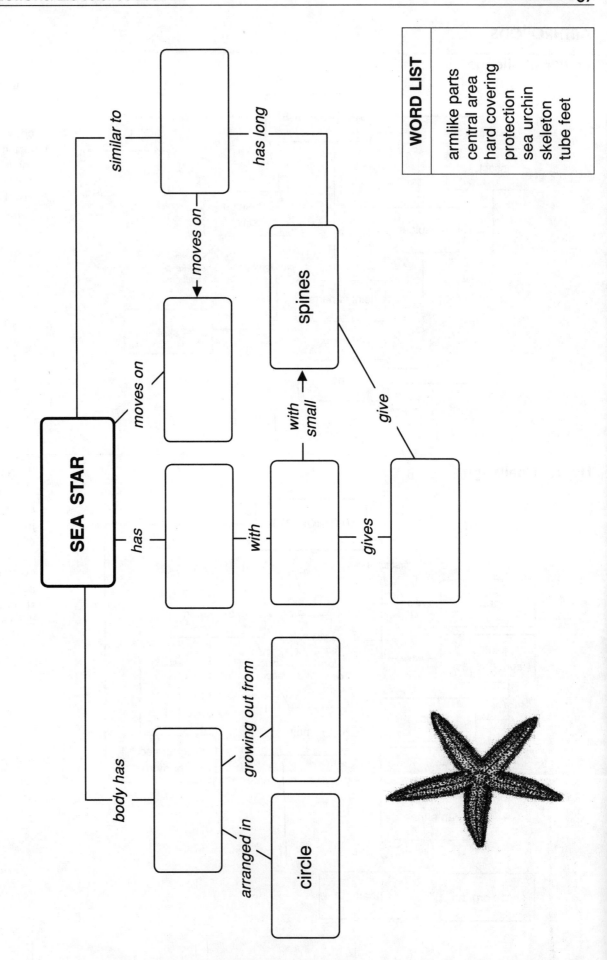

SEA STAR

similar to

moves on

has long

moves on

spines

has

with small

give

with

gives

body has

growing out from

arranged in

circle

Concept Map: Echinoderms

Directions: Select words from the word list and fill in the blank map items. Use each word only once, and use all the words on the list. Cut out the pictures in the picture gallery and paste or tape them in the correct boxes.

Name _____
Date _____   Period _____

© 2001 Critical Thinking Books & Software • www.criticalthinking.com • (800) 458-4849   89

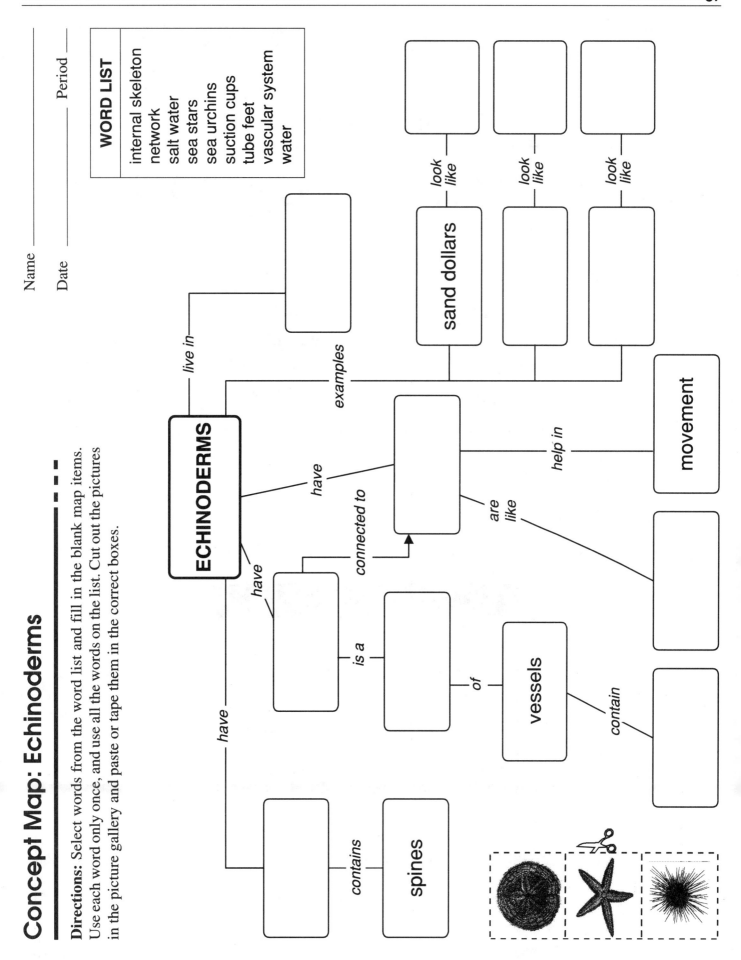

WORD LIST

internal skeleton
network
salt water
sea stars
sea urchins
suction cups
tube feet
vascular system
water

ECHINODERMS

live in

examples

have

have

have

connected to

is a

of

are like

help in

contains

sand dollars

look like

look like

look like

movement

vessels

contain

spines

Critical Thinking → C♥NCEPT FILE

Echinoderms

Characteristics

- internal skeleton with spines that often stick out through the skin

- skin has a hard covering that protects the animal and covers the skeleton

- body arranged in a circle with a center and armlike body parts that grow outward from the center

- live in sea water

Vocabulary

- ❑ **tube feet**—small tubes with suction cups that enable the animal to stick to a surface as it moves around

- ❑ **vascular system**—a network of vessels that contain water. It moves materials through the animal and is connected to the tube feet.

Examples

- sea stars—used to be called starfish, are in the shape of a star

- sand dollars—are flat and round

- sea urchins—are round and have long spines

ECHINODERMS

Lower Challenge

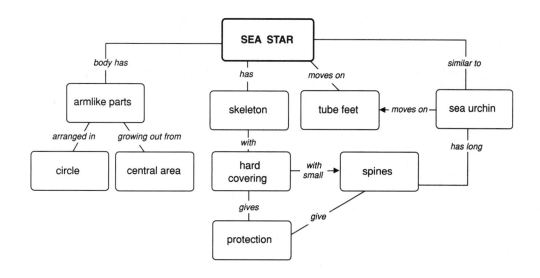

Score: 6 words

Starting hints: The seed item *spines* and connector *give* point to *protection*, and back to item *hard covering*.

The seed item *circle* suggests body structure.

Higher Challenge

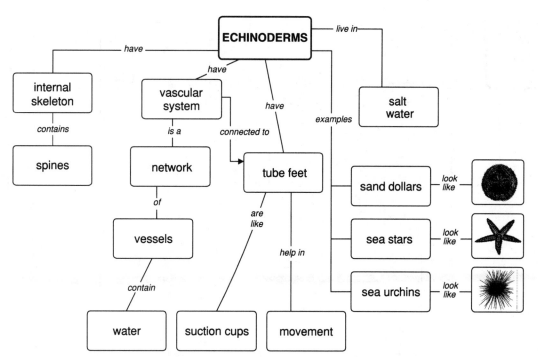

Score: 12 (9 words and 3 pictures)

Starting hints: The seed item *vessels* on the lower left suggests *network* and *vascular system* above.

The seed item *movement* points back to *tube feet*.

Pictures should match the correct label.

Concept Map: Vertebrates

Name _____

Date _____   Period _____

Directions: Select words from the word list and fill in the blank map items. Use each word only once, and use all the words on the list. Cut out the pictures in the picture gallery and paste or tape them in the correct boxes.

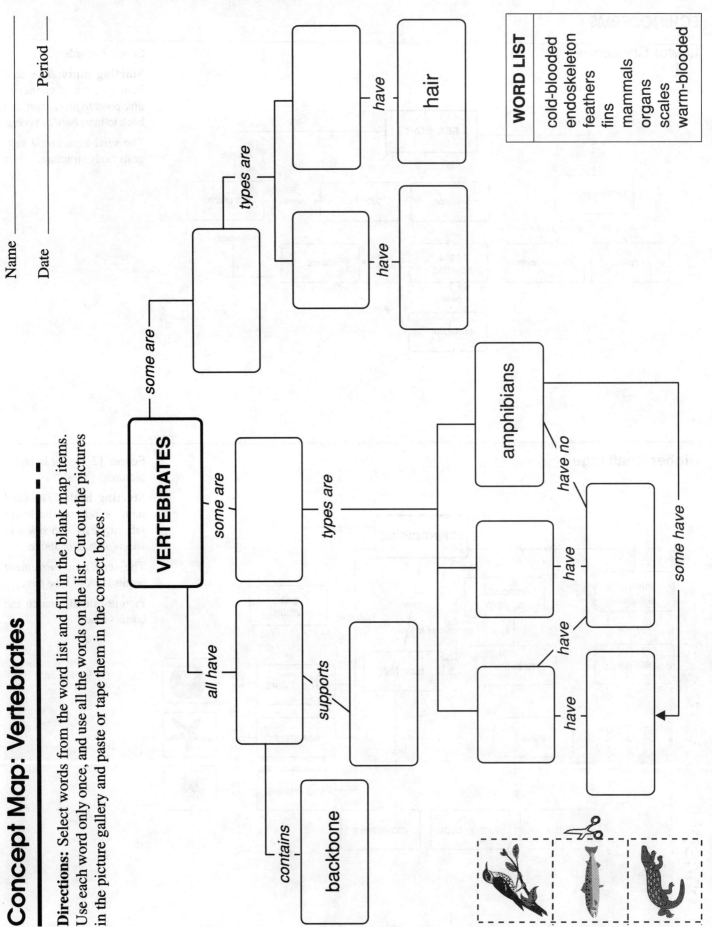

WORD LIST

cold-blooded
endoskeleton
feathers
fins
mammals
organs
scales
warm-blooded

VERTEBRATES

some are

all have

some are

types are

contains

supports

backbone

types are

amphibians

have no

have

have

have

some have

have

types are

have

hair

have

Name _____

Date _____   Period _____

Concept Map: Vertebrates

Directions: Select words from the word list and fill in the blank map items.
Use each word only once, and use all the words on the list. Cut out the pictures
in the picture gallery and paste or tape them in the correct boxes.

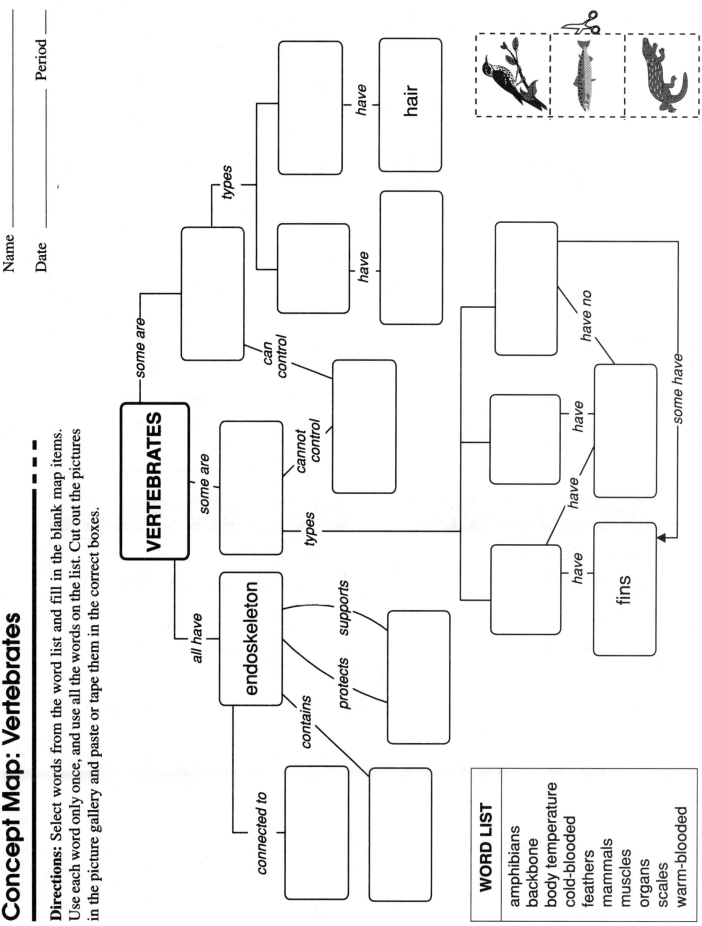

VERTEBRATES

some are

types

have

hair

have

can control

cannot control

some are

types

have no

have

have

have

some have

fins

all have

endoskeleton

supports

protects

contains

connected to

WORD LIST

amphibians
backbone
body temperature
cold-blooded
feathers
mammals
muscles
organs
scales
warm-blooded

Critical Thinking →

Vertebrates

Characteristics

All have an endoskeleton that
- protects the body organs.
- supports the body organs.
- includes a backbone.

Some are warm-blooded.

Some are cold-blooded.

Vocabulary

❑ **cold-blooded**—animals whose body temperature changes with the outside temperature

❑ **endoskeleton**—skeleton on the inside of an animal's body; muscles attached to it

❑ **warm-blooded**—animals whose body temperature is kept constant

Warm-blooded Types

- Mammals
  - have hair
- Birds
  - have feathers

Cold-blooded Types

- Fish
  - have scales and fins
- Reptiles
  - have scales
- Amphibians
  - have no scales; some have fins

VERTEBRATES

Lower Challenge

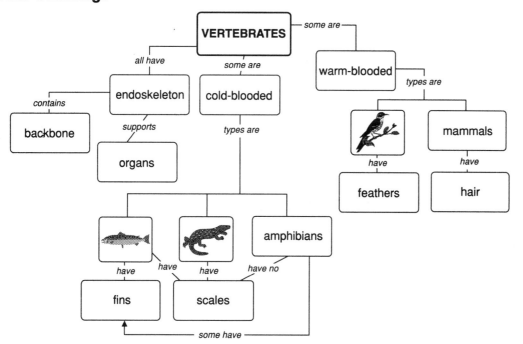

Score: 11 (8 words and 3 pictures)

Starting hints: The item *hair* points to the item *mammals* above it (on the right side). Since mammals are warm-blooded, the item *warm-blooded* goes above *mammals*.

Fish and reptiles have scales, but amphibians do not (lower center).

Higher Challenge

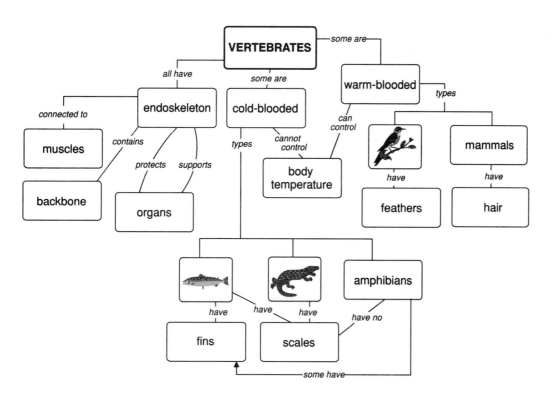

Score: 13 (10 words and 3 pictures)

Starting hints: See notes for map above.

Name _____

Date _____

Period _____

Concept Map: Warm-blooded Vertebrates

Directions: Select words from the word list to fill in the blank map items.
Use each word only once, and use all the words on the list.

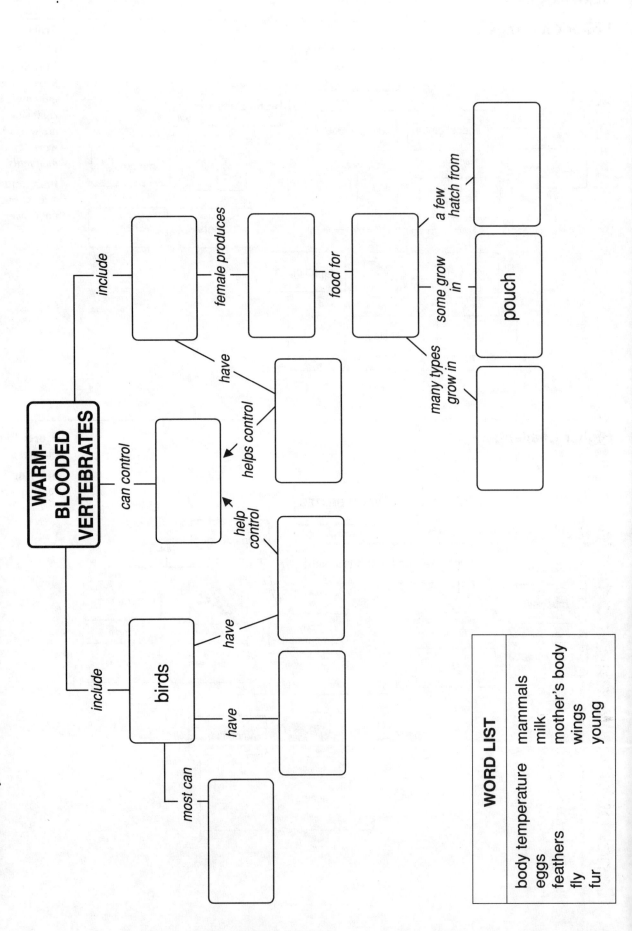

WORD LIST

body temperature	mammals
eggs	milk
feathers	mother's body
fly	wings
fur	young

Name _____

Date _____

Period _____

Concept Map: Warm-blooded Vertebrates

Directions: Select words from the word list to fill in the blank map items.
Use each word only once, and use all the words on the list.

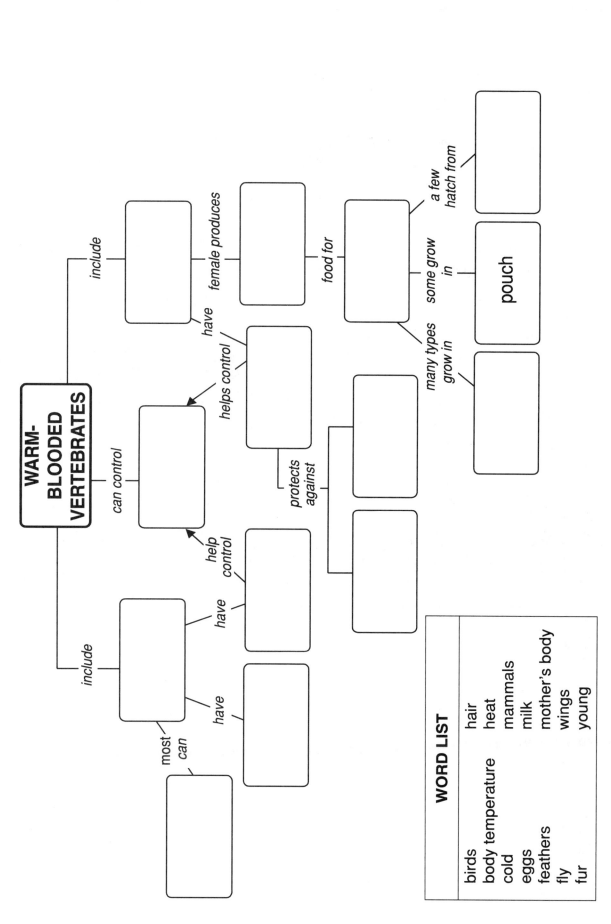

WORD LIST

birds	hair
body temperature	heat
cold	mammals
eggs	milk
feathers	mother's body
fly	wings
fur	young

Critical Thinking →

Warm-blooded Vertebrates

Mammals

Mammals are warm-blooded vertebrates. They have hair. The hair helps their bodies keep a constant body temperature.

Female mammals produce milk, which they feed to the young.

The young of a few mammals hatch from eggs.

Some mammal young grow in their mother's pouch.

Most mammal young grow inside the mother's body.

Vocabulary

☐ **warm-blooded**—the ability to control inside body temperature

☐ **vertebrate**—an animal with a backbone

Birds

Birds are warm-blooded vertebrates. They have feathers. The feathers help their bodies keep an unchanging temperature.

Birds have wings, and most have the ability to fly.

WARM-BLOODED VERTEBRATES

Lower Challenge

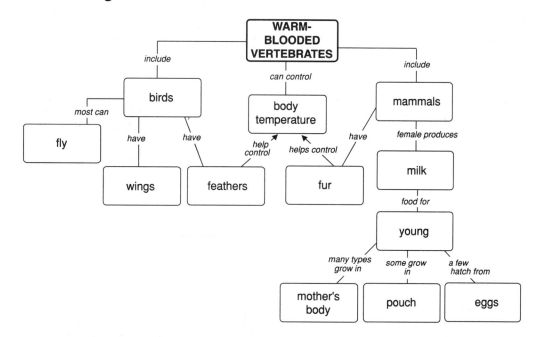

Score: 10 words

Starting hints: The connector-item combination *some grow in pouch* at the lower right points to *young*. The central connector, *can control*, points to *body temperature*.

Higher Challenge

Score: 13 words

Starting hints: See notes above.

Concept Map: Cold-blooded Vertebrates

Directions: Select words from the word list to fill in the blank map items.
Use each word only once, and use all the words on the list.

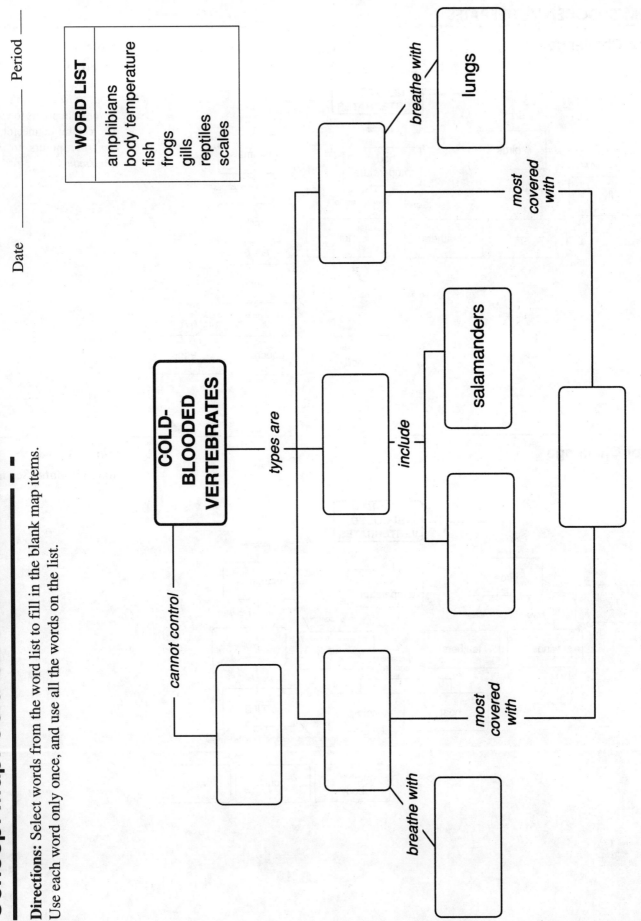

WORD LIST

amphibians
body temperature
fish
frogs
gills
reptiles
scales

COLD-
BLOODED
VERTEBRATES

cannot control

types are

include

salamanders

breathe with

most covered with

breathe with

lungs

most covered with

Concept Map: Cold-blooded Vertebrates

Directions: Select words from the word list to fill in the blank map items.
Use each word only once, and use all the words on the list.

Name _____

Date _____   Period _____

WORD LIST

amphibians	lungs
body temperature	oxygen
fish	protection
gills	reptiles
in water	scales

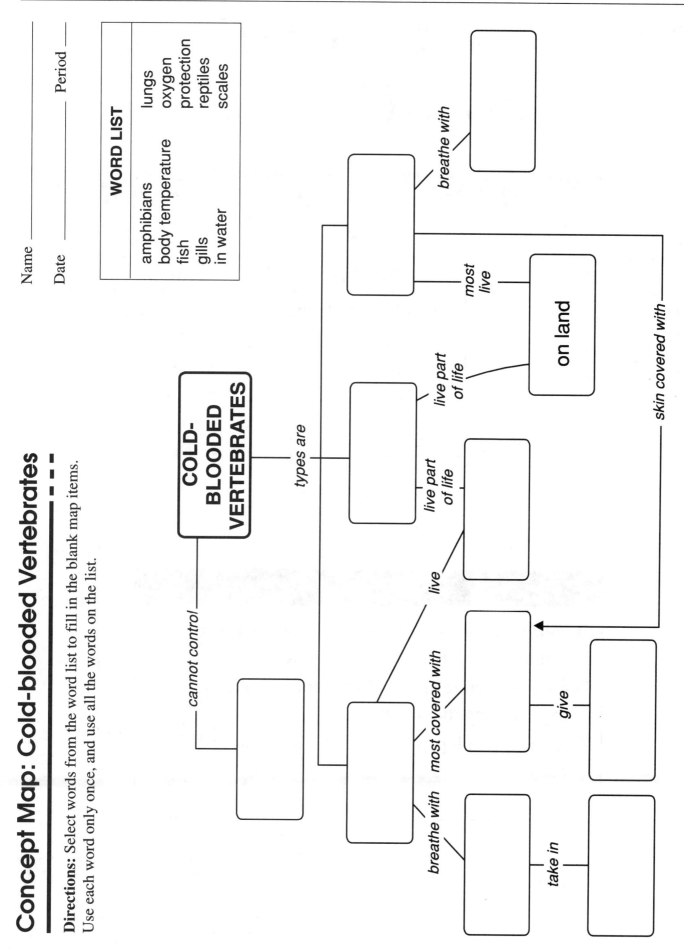

Critical Thinking

Cold-blooded Vertebrates

Major Types

Fish	**Reptiles**	**Amphibians**

• breathe with gills
• live in the water
• are covered with scales
	• breathe with lungs
	• many live on land
	• are covered with scales
		• young live in water; adults live on land
		• include:
		  – frogs
		  – toads
		  – salamanders

Vocabulary

❏ **cold-blooded**—means that an animal cannot control its inside body temperature

❏ **gills**—structures that help the animal take in oxygen from the water

❏ **scales**—tough parts of the skin that protect the body

COLD-BLOODED VERTEBRATES

Lower Challenge

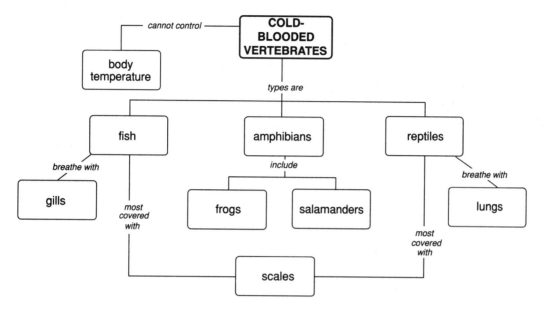

Score: 7 words

Starting hints: The only group of cold-blooded vertebrates that breathe solely with *lungs* is the *reptiles*.

Salamanders are an example of the *amphibians*. This leaves the fish group for the left side.

Higher Challenge

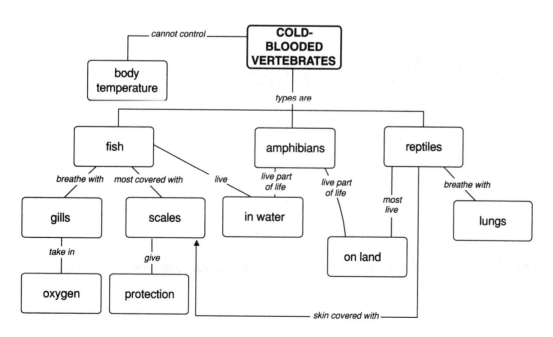

Score: 10 words

Starting hints: Start at the bottom center with the item *on land*. The connector *live part of life* suggests *amphibians*. The connector *most live* suggests *reptiles*.

Concept Map: Metamorphosis

Name _____

Date _____ Period ____

Directions: Select words from the word list to fill in the blank map items. Use each word only once, and use all the words on the list.

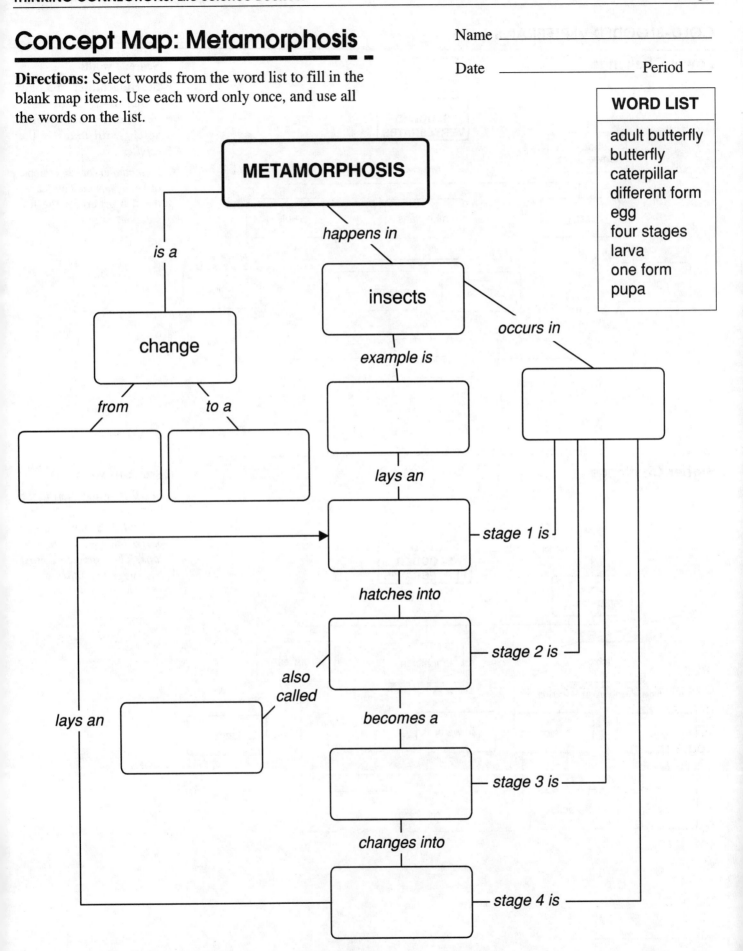

WORD LIST

adult butterfly
butterfly
caterpillar
different form
egg
four stages
larva
one form
pupa

Concept Map: Metamorphosis

Name _____

Date _____ Period ____

Directions: Select words from the word list to fill in the blank map items. Use each word only once, and use all the words on the list. Then use two different highlighters, colored pencils, or crayons to color in items that are (1) related to insects and (2) related to frogs. Show your color scheme in the legend.

COLOR LEGEND

☐	Related to insects
☐	Related to frogs

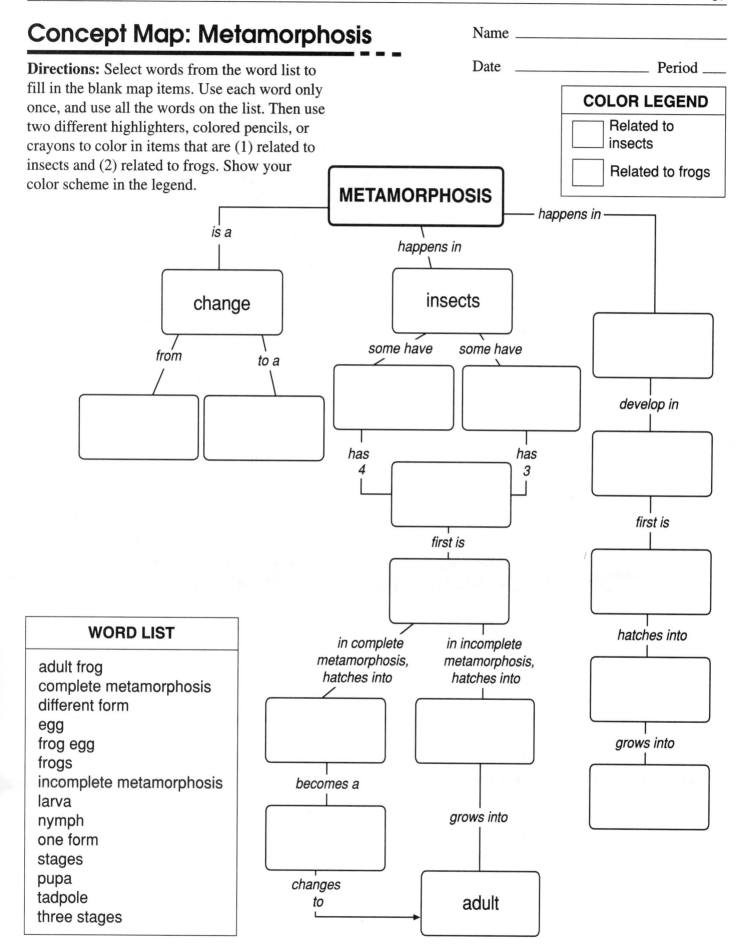

WORD LIST

adult frog
complete metamorphosis
different form
egg
frog egg
frogs
incomplete metamorphosis
larva
nymph
one form
stages
pupa
tadpole
three stages

Critical Thinking → C◯NCEPT FILE

Metamorphosis

What Is Metamorphosis?

Metamorphosis is a *change*

- happens in some animals
- change is from one form to another

Vocabulary

❐ **larva**—the young stage in *complete* metamorphosis, grows from the egg. In some animals is called the caterpillar.

❐ **nymph**—the middle stage of *incomplete* metamorphosis

❐ **pupa**—the resting stage of complete metamorphosis between the larva and the adult

Insects

Insects have two types of metamorphosis.

Complete

Has four stages:

- egg
- larva
- pupa
- adult

Incomplete

Has three stages:

- egg
- nymph
- adult

Amphibians

Frogs and all amphibians have three stages of metamorphosis:

- egg
- tadpole
- adult

METAMORPHOSIS

Lower Challenge

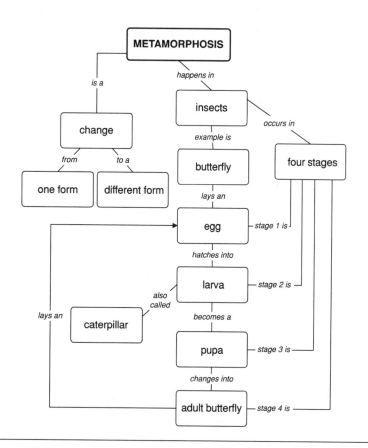

Score: 9 words

Starting hints: The connector *lays an* strongly suggests *egg*. The rest will follow in sequence.

Higher Challenge

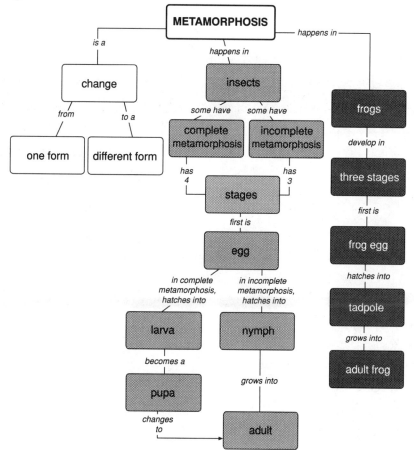

Score: 28 (14 words and 14 correct color coding)

Starting hints: The three connectors that include the phrase *hatches into* point to *larva*, *nymph*, and *tadpole*. The line on the right deals with frogs, as the central line is insects.

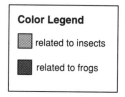

Color Legend

☐ related to insects

■ related to frogs

Concept Map: Nervous System

Name ———————

Date ———————   Period ———

Directions: Select words from the word list and fill in the blank map items.
Use each word only once, and use all the words on the list.

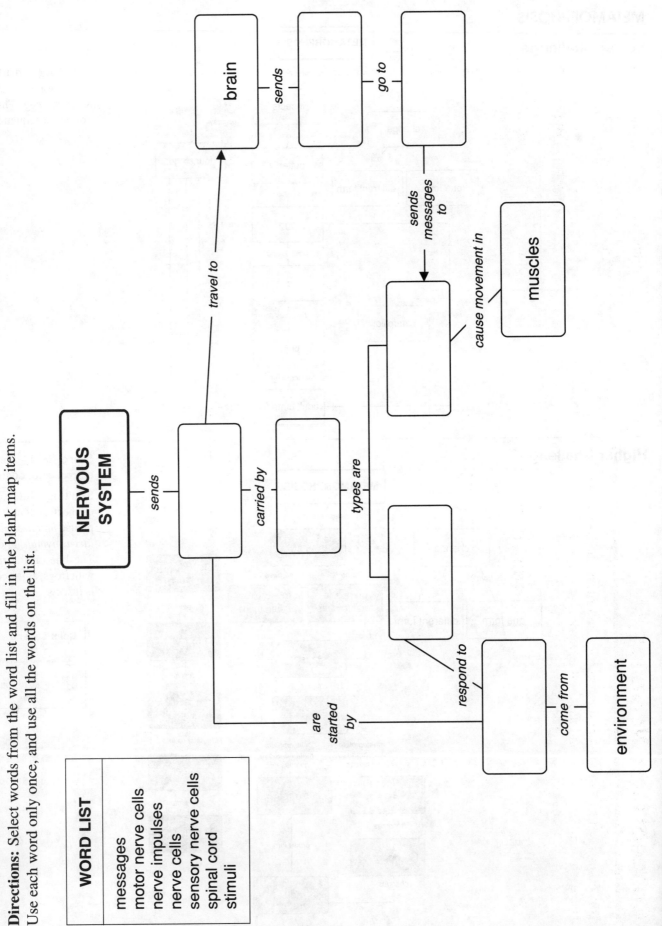

WORD LIST

messages
motor nerve cells
nerve impulses
nerve cells
sensory nerve cells
spinal cord
stimuli

Concept Map: Nervous System

Name _____

Date _____ Period _____

Directions: Select words from the word list and fill in the blank map items.
Use each word only once, and use all the words on the list.

WORD LIST

brain	nerve impulses
environment	neurons
messages	sensory neurons
motor neurons	spinal cord
muscles	stimuli

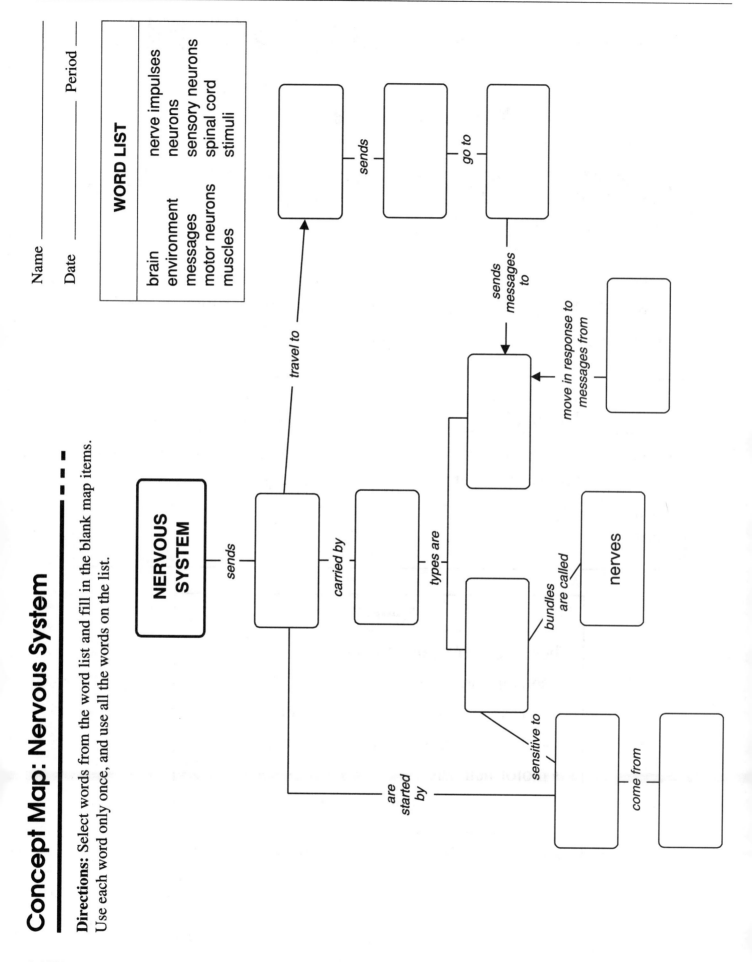

 **C NCEPT FILE**

Nervous System

Parts

The nervous system is made up of:

- the brain
- the spinal cord
- neurons

Vocabulary

- ☐ **neurons**—the cells that carry nerve impulses
- ☐ **stimuli**—plural of stimulus, things such as light, sound, etc., in the environment

The Brain

- receives nerve impulses from the body's nervous system
- sends messages to the spinal cord

The Spinal Cord

- receives message from the brain
- sends messages to the motor neurons

Neurons

There are two kinds of neurons:

- sensory neurons
  - respond to stimuli from the environment
  - bundles of these are called "nerves"
- motor neurons
  - get message from the spinal cord
  - cause muscles to move

NERVOUS SYSTEM

Lower Challenge

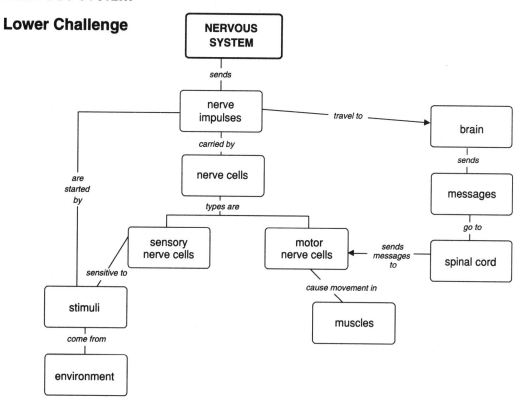

Score: 7 words

Starting hints: The item *brain* on the upper right is a good place to start. The connector *sends* suggests the item *messages*.

The connector-item combination *cause movement in muscles* points back to *motor nerve cells*.

Higher Challenge

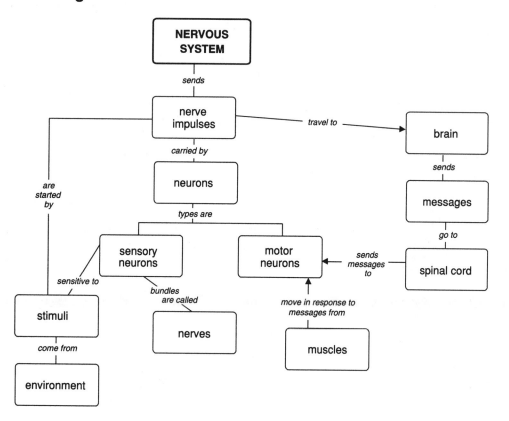

Score: 10 words

Starting hints: The two maps are very similar, but the vocabulary for the challenging map is more advanced. See hints above.

Concept Map: The Brain

Name _____

Date _____   Period _____

Directions: Select words from the word list and fill in the blank map items.
Use each word only once, and use all the words on the list.

WORD LIST

body parts	medulla
breathing	sense of balance
cerebellum	senses
cerebrum	skull
emotions	spinal column
heartbeat	

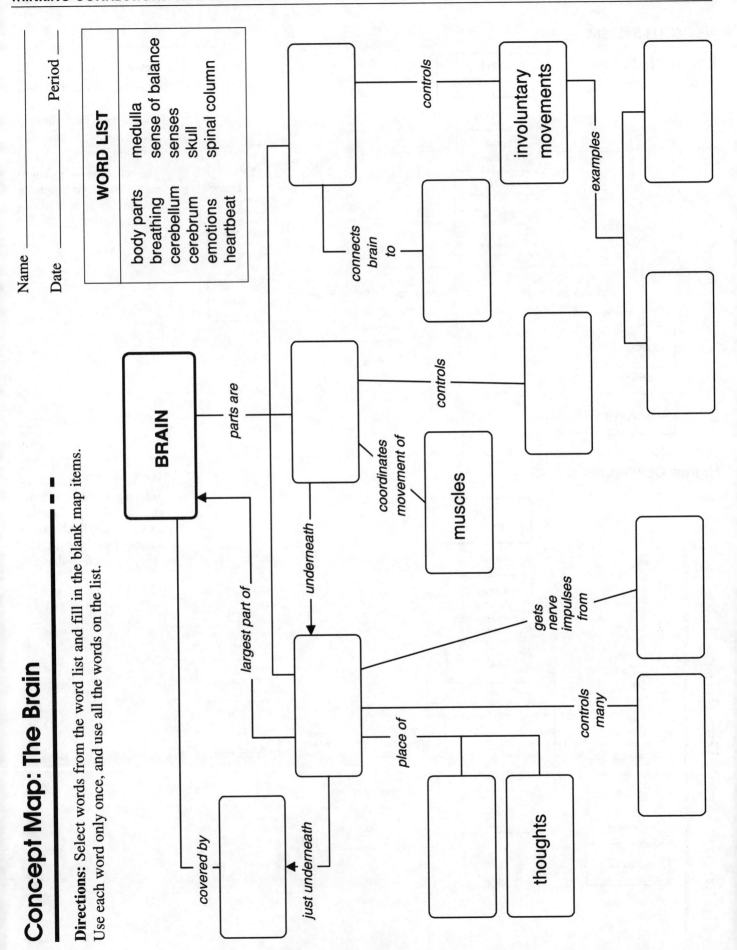

Concept Map: The Brain

Directions: Select words from the word list and fill in the blank map items.
Use each word only once, and use all the words on the list.

WORD LIST

involuntary movements	attitudes
medulla	blinking
muscles	body parts
sense of balance	breathing
senses	cerebellum
skull	cerebrum
spinal column	emotions

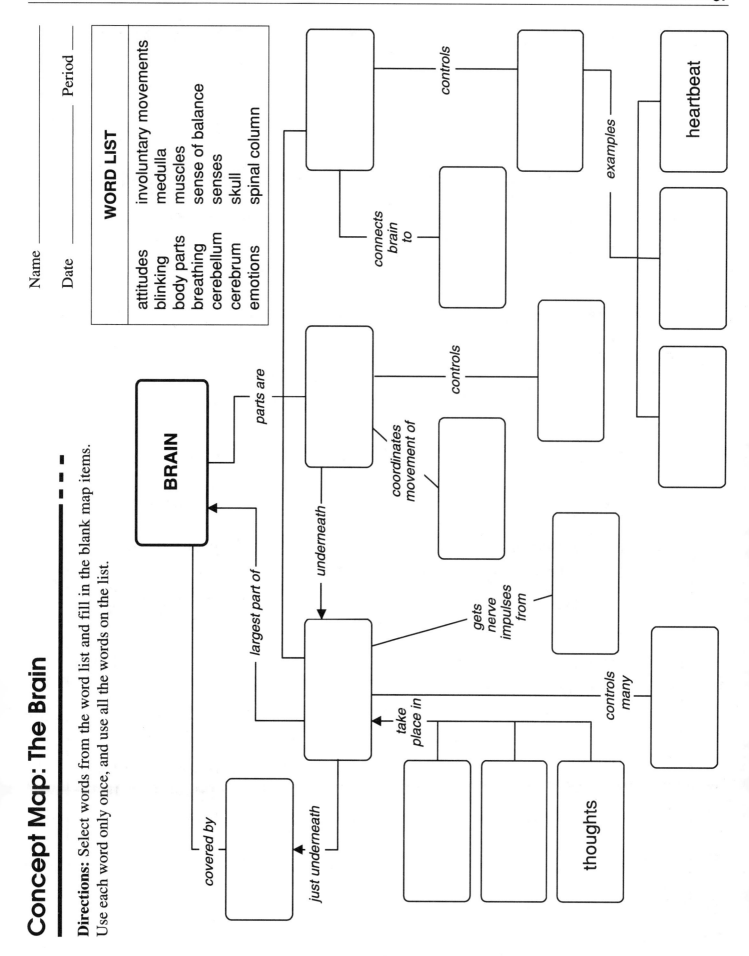

Critical Thinking →  C NCEPT FILE

The Brain

Structure

The brain has three main parts:
- cerebellum
- cerebrum
- medulla

Vocabulary

- ❑ **involuntary movements**— movements that a person normally cannot control, such as the beating of the heart
- ❑ **senses**—the ability of a person to detect the world through seeing, hearing, touching, tasting, and smelling

Medulla

- connects the brain to the spinal column
- controls involuntary movements, such as
  - blinking
  - breathing

Cerebellum

- coordinates movements of muscles
- controls balance

Cerebrum

- largest part of the brain
- is just under the skull
- controls many parts of the body
- receives impulses from the senses
- attitudes, emotions, and thoughts all happen here

THE BRAIN

Lower Challenge

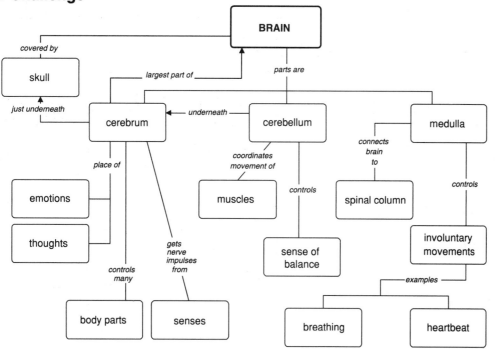

Score: 11 words

Starting hints: The item on the lower right, *involuntary movements*, suggests the medulla above it.

On the lower left, the connector-item combination *place of thoughts* suggests the item *cerebrum*.

Higher Challenge

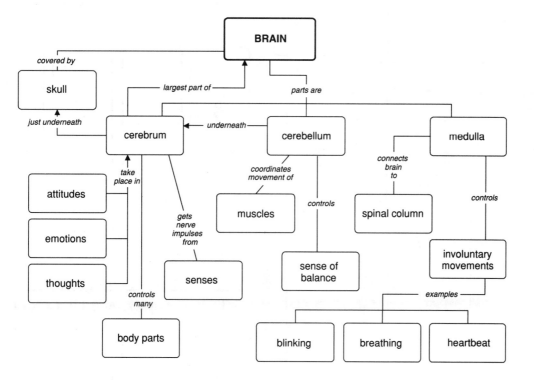

Score: 14 words

Starting hints: On the lower right, the item *heartbeat* is an involuntary movement.

On the left, the connector-item combination *thoughts take place in* suggests the item *cerebrum*.

Concept Map: The Senses

Directions: Select words from the word list and fill in the blank map items.
Use each word only once, and use all the words on the list.

Name _____

Date _____   Period _____

WORD LIST

bitter	heat	salty	sweet
cold	inner ear	sight	taste
eardrum	pressure	skin	taste buds
eye	retina	smell	touch
hearing			

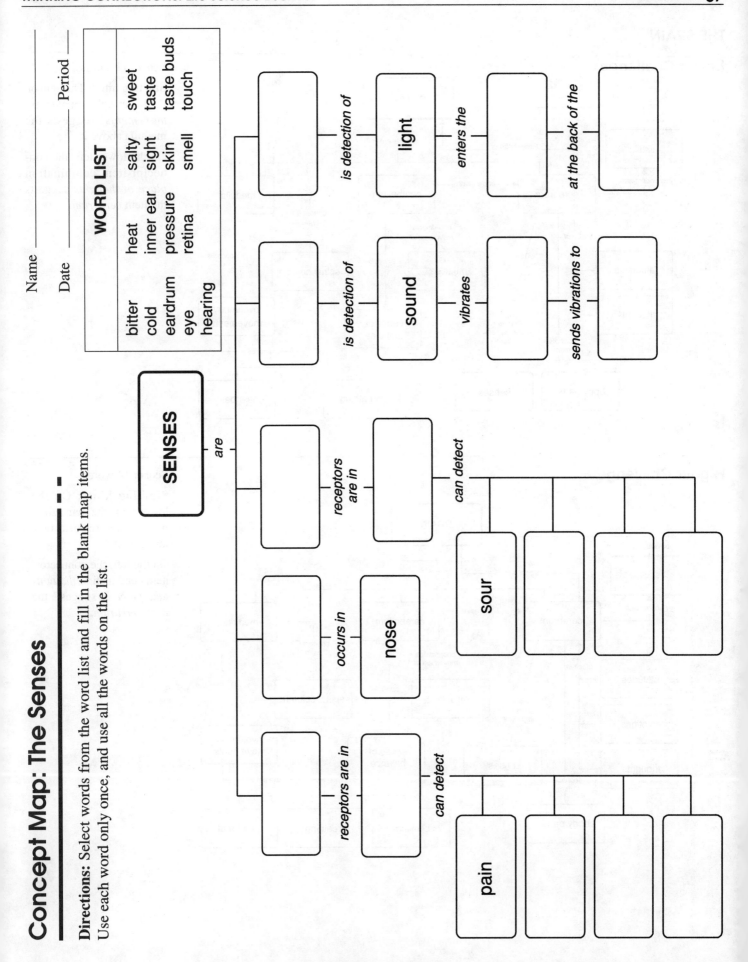

SENSES

are

is detection of — light — *enters the* — *at the back of the*

is detection of — sound — *vibrates* — *sends vibrations to*

receptors are in — *can detect* — sour

occurs in — nose

receptors are in — *can detect* — pain

Concept Map: The Senses

Directions: Select words from the word list and fill in the blank map items.
Use each word only once, and use all the words on the list.

Name _____

Date _____ Period _____

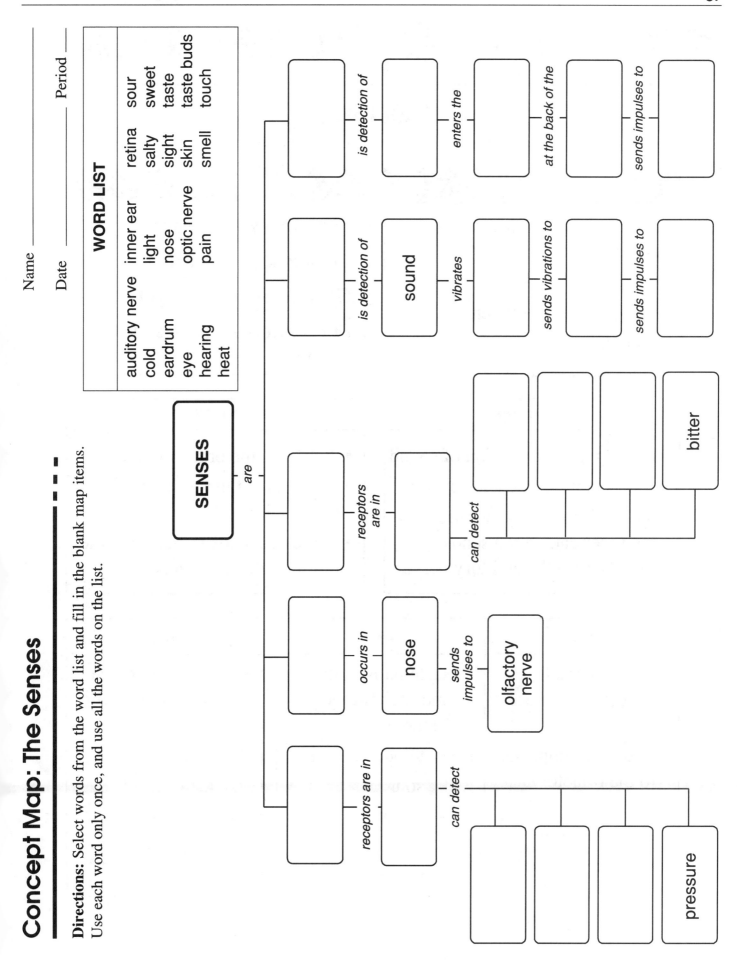

WORD LIST

auditory nerve	inner ear	retina	sour
cold	light	salty	sweet
eardrum	nose	sight	taste
eye	optic nerve	skin	taste buds
hearing	pain	smell	touch
heat			

SENSES

are

is detection of — enters the — at the back of the — sends impulses to

is detection of — sound — vibrates — sends vibrations to — sends impulses to

receptors are in — can detect — bitter

occurs in — nose — sends impulses to — olfactory nerve

receptors are in — can detect — pressure

Critical Thinking ➡ CNCEPT FILE

Senses

Types	Vocabulary
There are five main types of senses: • hearing • taste • sight • touch • smell	❏ **auditory**—related to hearing ❏ **olfactory**—related to smelling ❏ **optic**—related to sight ❏ **receptor**—nerve that detects stimuli

Hearing	Sight
• hearing is the detection of sound • sound vibrates the eardrum • the eardrum sends vibrations to the inner ear, which sends impulses on the auditory nerve	• the eye is the organ of sight • the retina, at the back of the eye, detects light • the retina sends impulses to the brain by the optic nerve

Smell	Taste	Touch

• sense of smell occurs in the nose
 • detectors in the nose send impulses to the olfactory nerve
	• taste buds in the mouth hold the receptors
	 • taste buds detect
	    – sour
	    – sweet
	    – salty
	    – bitter
		• touch receptors are located in the skin
		 • they can detect
		    – pain
		    – heat
		    – cold
		    – pressure

THE SENSES

Lower Challenge

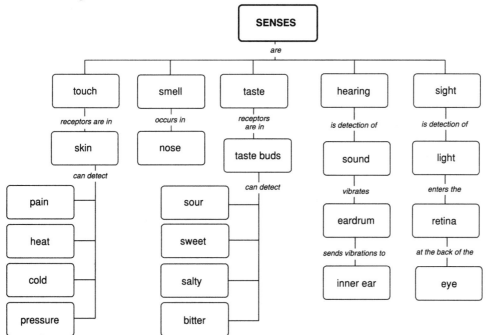

Score: 17 words

Starting hints: The items *sound* and *light* point back to hearing and sight respectively. The seed item *pain* suggests the item skin, which also points to heat, cold, and pressure. The latter items are interchangeable. The items under *sour* are also interchangeable.

Each sense, and its related boxes, could be colored for emphasis.

Higher Challenge

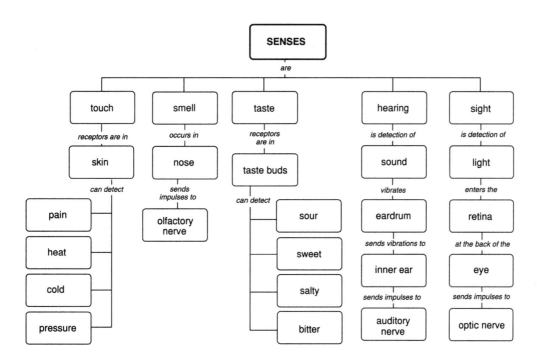

Score: 20 words

Starting hints: The item *sound* points back to hearing. The item *olfactory nerve* suggests nose and smell.

Name _____

Date _____ Period _____

Concept Map: The Skin

Directions: Select words from the word list and fill in the blank map items.
Use each word only once, and use all the words on the list.

WORD LIST

dead cells	oil glands
fat	pain
heat	pores
nerves	sweat
oil	sweat glands

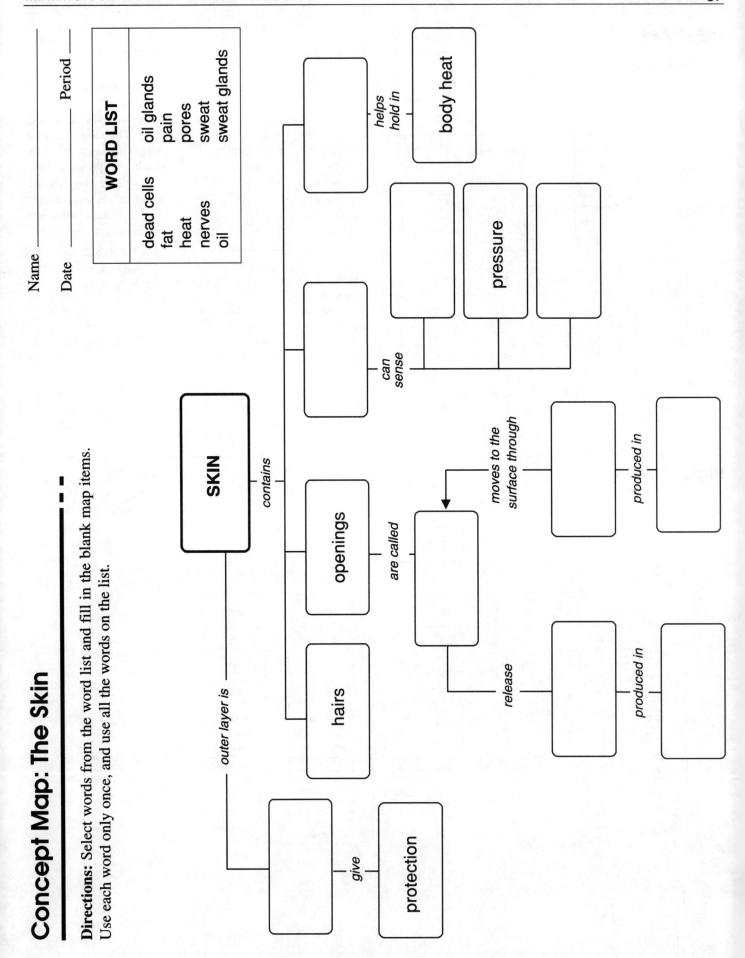

Concept Map: The Skin

Directions: Select words from the word list and fill in the blank map items.
Use each word only once, and use all the words on the list.

WORD LIST

dead cells	oil
epidermis	oil glands
fat	pain
follicles	pores
heat	sweat
nerves	sweat glands

Name _____ Period _____

Date _____

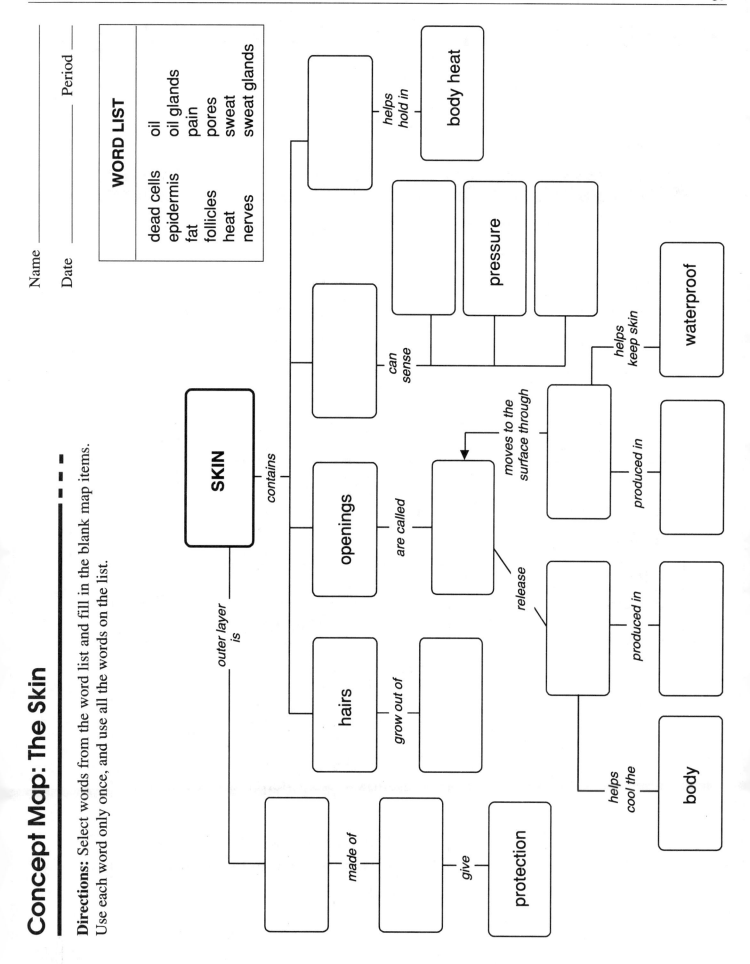

SKIN

contains

outer layer *is*

helps hold in → **body heat**

can sense

pressure

openings *are called*

moves to the surface through

helps keep skin → **waterproof**

produced in

release

produced in

hairs *grow out of*

helps cool the → **body**

made of

give → **protection**

Critical Thinking ⟶

The Skin

Structure

Skin is the largest organ of the human body. It contains

- nerves
- openings
- hairs
- fat

Vocabulary

- ❏ **epidermis**—the protective outer layer of skin made of dead cells
- ❏ **follicle**—the part of the skin that grows hair

Nerves

The nerves in the skin can sense

- heat
- pain
- pressure

Fat

Fat in the skin helps the body hold in heat.

Hair

Hair grows out of the follicles.

Openings

The openings in skin are called "pores."

The skin uses pores in two ways:

- to release sweat from sweat glands. Sweat helps to cool the body.
- to release oil made in oil glands. Oil helps to keep the skin water-proof.

THE SKIN

Lower Challenge

Score: 10 words

Starting hints: The connector *can sense* suggests the item *nerves*. The two sense stimuli, heat and pain, can be listed in either order.

The answers on the left dealing with sweat and oil might be answered either way, as both substances move to the surface through pores.

On the extreme left, dead cells give protection.

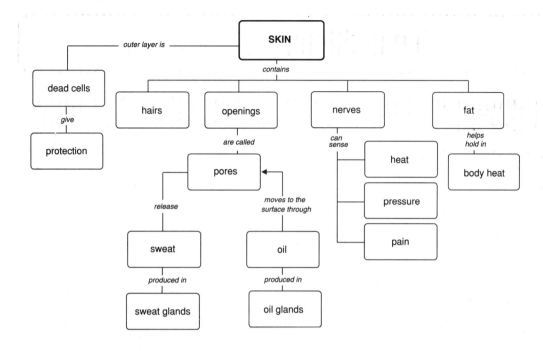

Higher Challenge

Score: 12 words

Starting hints: The notes to the above map will help as clues for students starting out.

In this map, the section on sweat and oil has more information. Sweat helps cool the body and oil helps keep the skin waterproof.

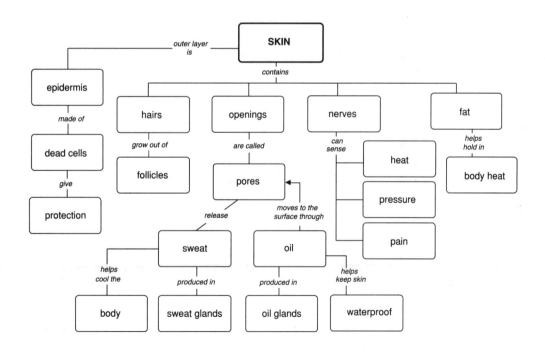

Concept Map: The Skeletal System

Directions: Select words from the word list and fill in the blank map items. Use each word only once, and use all the words on the list.

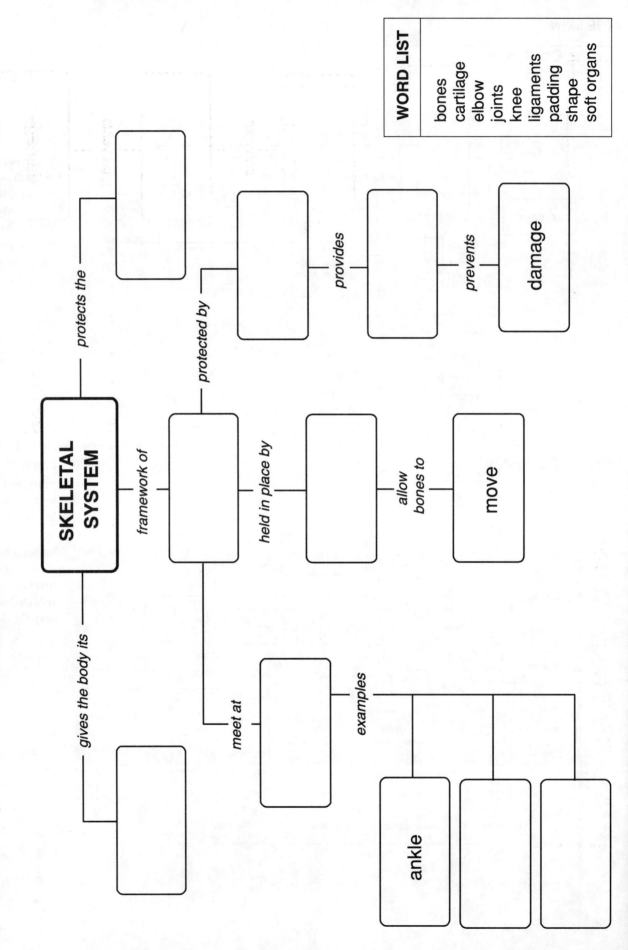

WORD LIST

bones
cartilage
elbow
joints
knee
ligaments
padding
shape
soft organs

Concept Map: The Skeletal System

Directions: Select words from the word list and fill in the blank map items. Use each word only once, and use all the words on the list.

Name _____

Date _____

Period _____

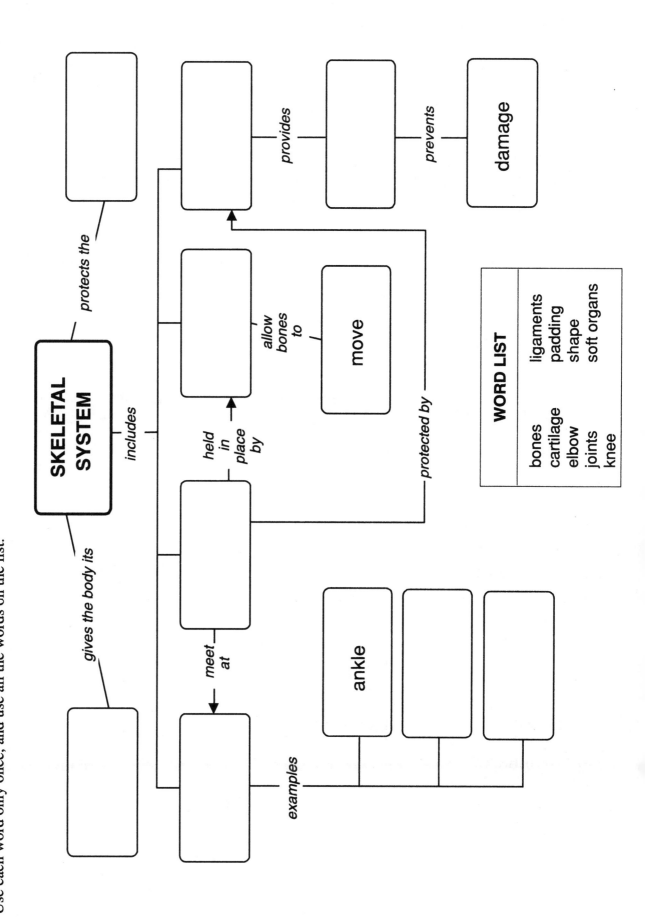

WORD LIST

bones	ligaments
cartilage	padding
elbow	shape
joints	soft organs
knee	

SKELETAL SYSTEM

protects the

provides

prevents

damage

gives the body its

includes

allow bones to

move

held in place by

protected by

meet at

examples

ankle

Critical Thinking

The Skeletal System

Parts	Vocabulary
The skeletal system includes: • joints • bones • ligaments • cartilage	☐ **cartilage**—a thick, tough, flexible tissue softer than bone ☐ **ligament**—a tough band of fiber

Functions

The skeletal system gives shape to the body and protects the soft organs inside.

Joints	Ligaments	Cartilage

• occur where bones meet bones
• examples are
  – ankle
  – knee
  – elbow
	• hold bones in place
	• allow bones to move
		• protect bones
		  – prevent damage
		  – provide padding

THE SKELETAL SYSTEM

Lower Challenge

Score: 9 words

Starting hints: The item on the lower right, *damage*, suggests padding above it.

On the lower left, the connector *examples* and item *ankle* point to knee and elbow, which can be put in either order.

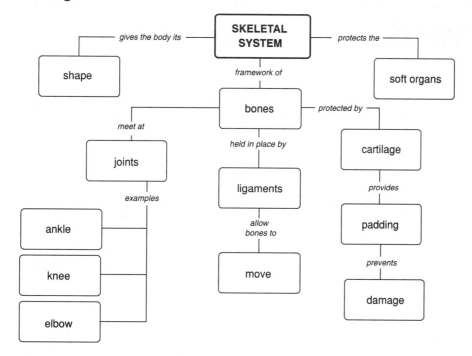

Higher Challenge

Score: 12 words

Starting hints: See notes above.

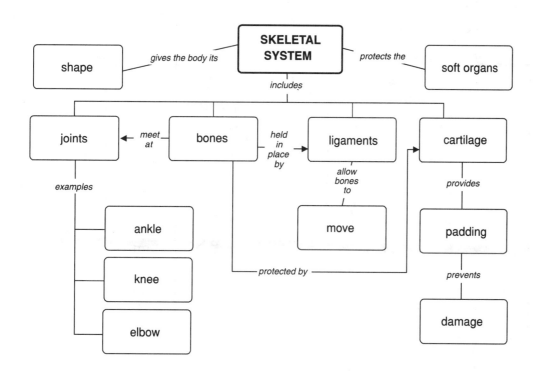

Concept Map: Bone

Name _____

Date _____

Period _____

WORD LIST

hollow spaces
marrow
outer layer
shock absorber
solid bone
spongy bone
strength

Directions: Select words from the word list and fill in the blank map items.
Use each word only once, and use all the words on the list.

BONE

inner layer is

makes

blood cells

surrounds

third layer is

contains

help keep bones from

breaking

act as

second layer is

covers

gives the bone

structure is

covered by

covers

very hard

Concept Map: Bone

Name _____

Date _____   Period _____

Directions: Select words from the word list and fill in the blank map items. Use each word only once, and use all the words on the list.

WORD LIST

blood cells	shock absorber
breaking	solid bone
calcium	spongy bone
hollow spaces	strength
marrow	very hard
periosteum	

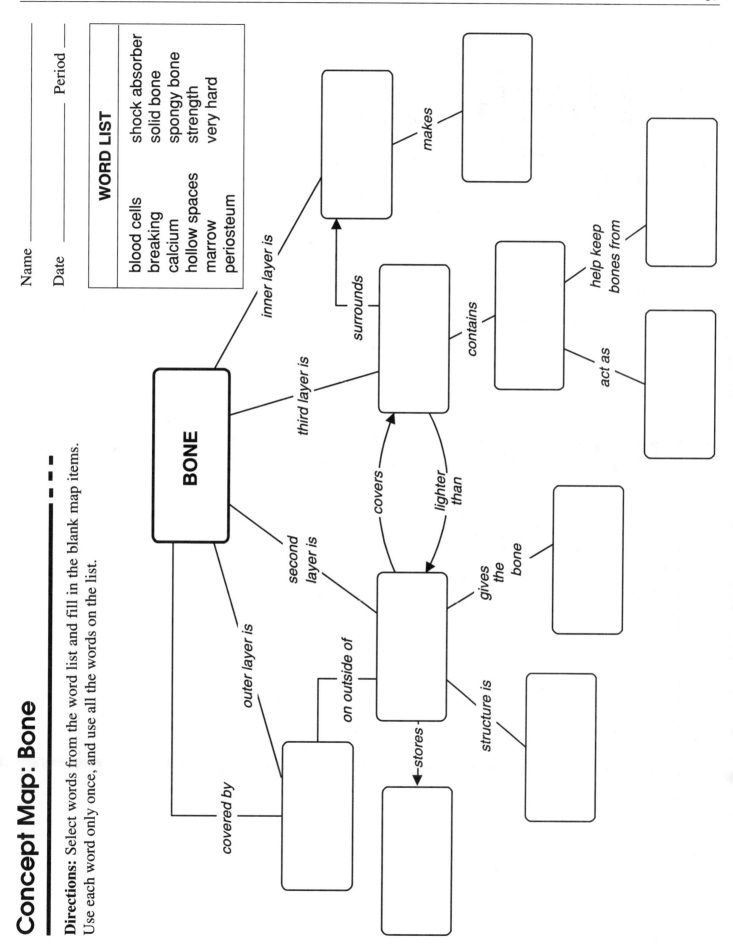

Critical Thinking ➔  CONCEPT FILE

Bone

Structure of bone	Vocabulary
Human bone has four layers: • outer layer • solid bone • spongy bone • marrow	☐ **marrow**—soft tissue in the center of the bone ☐ **periosteum**—a name for the outer layer of the bone

Four Layers

Outer layer	Solid bone	Spongy bone	Marrow
• covers the bone • protects the bone	• just under the outer layer • makes the bone strong • is very hard • calcium is stored here • covers the spongy bone	• contains hollow spaces • absorbs shocks • helps keep bone from breaking • lighter than solid bone	• found deep within bone • blood cells are made here

BONE

Lower Challenge

Score: 7 words

Starting hints: The item-connector combination of *makes* and *blood cells* on the lower right points to *marrow*.

The item on the lower left, *very hard*, describes the item *solid bone*.

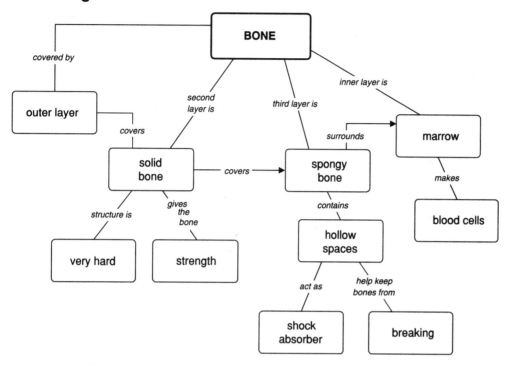

Higher Challenge

Score: 10 words

Starting hints: The connector *makes* on the lower right suggests manufacturing of something. The only product in the word list is *blood cells*, and the agent that makes them is *marrow*.

The item on the far lower left, *calcium*, is stored in the *solid bone*.

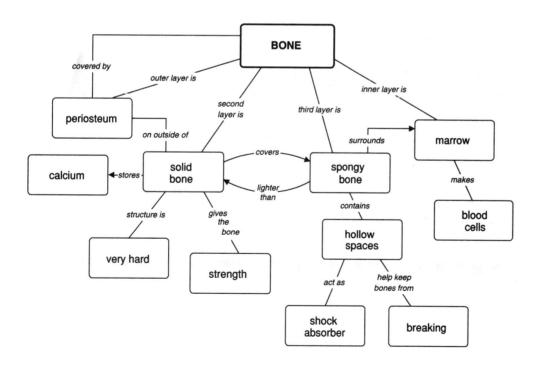

Name _____

Date _____   Period _____

Concept Map: Joints

Directions: Select words from the word list and fill in the blank map items.
Use each word only once, and use all the words on the list.

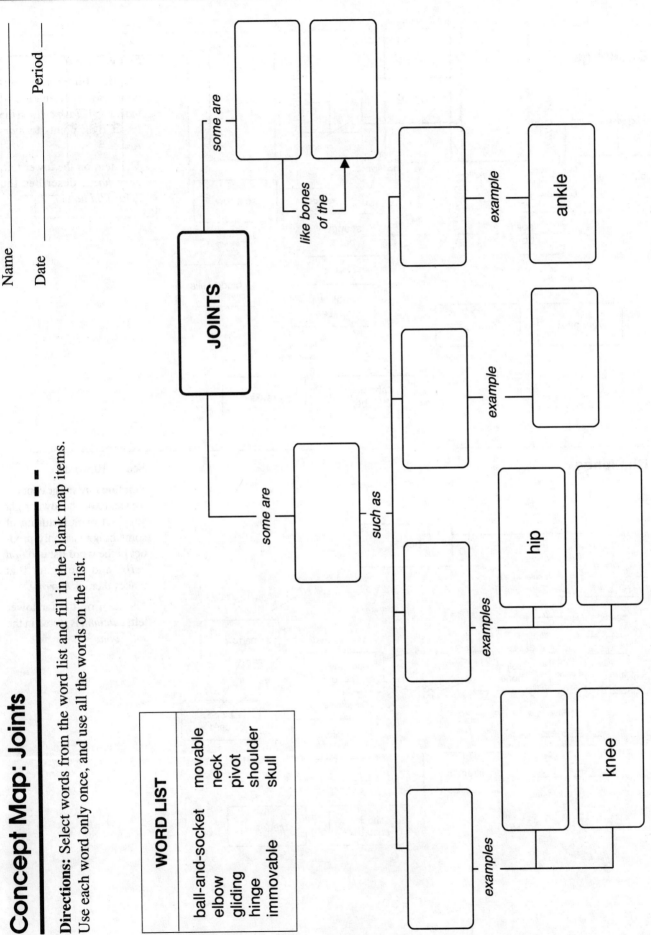

WORD LIST

ball-and-socket	movable
elbow	neck
gliding	pivot
hinge	shoulder
immovable	skull

Concept Map: Joints

Directions: Select words from the word list and fill in the blank map items.
Use each word only once, and use all the words on the list.

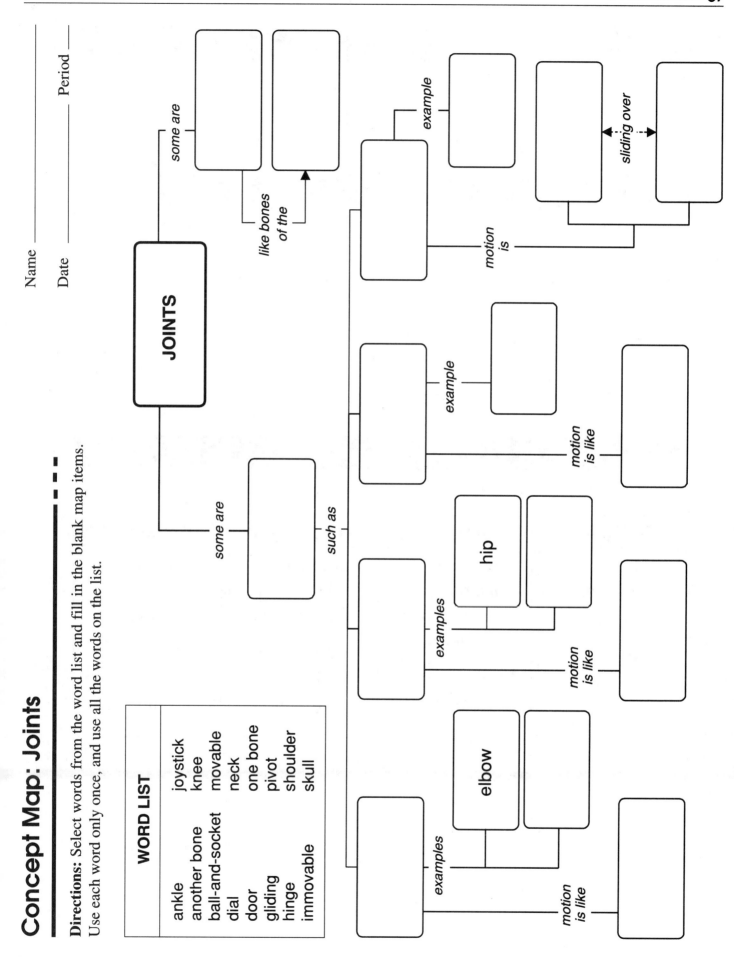

Critical Thinking ➔  C⚡NCEPT FILE

Joints

About joints

Joints are places where bone meets bone.

There are two kinds of joints:

- movable—there are four kinds
- immovable

Vocabulary

☐ **immovable**—something that cannot move. The bones of the skull meet at immovable joints.

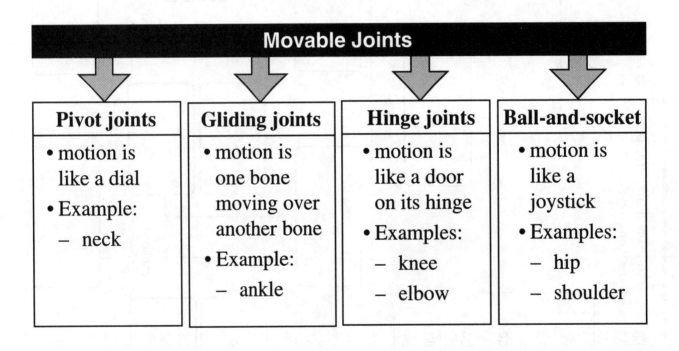

Movable Joints

Pivot joints

- motion is like a dial
- Example:
  - neck

Gliding joints

- motion is one bone moving over another bone
- Example:
  - ankle

Hinge joints

- motion is like a door on its hinge
- Examples:
  - knee
  - elbow

Ball-and-socket

- motion is like a joystick
- Examples:
  - hip
  - shoulder

JOINTS

Lower Challenge

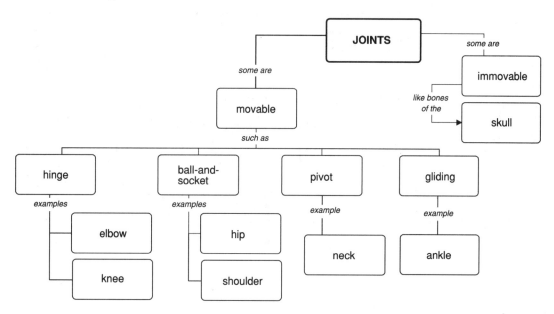

Score: 8 words

Starting hints: Three of the types of joints have an example given on the map. These should suggest the missing items.

Higher Challenge

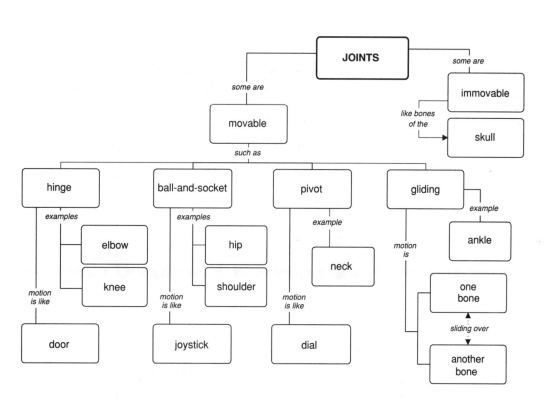

Score: 16 words

Starting hints: Two of the joints have examples given on the map. These should suggest the missing examples from the word list.

Concept Map: Muscles

Directions: Select words from the word list and fill in the blank map items. Use each word only once, and use all the words on the list.

Name _____

Date _____

Period _____

WORD LIST

biceps	fibers
bones	relax
cardiac muscles	skeletal muscles
contract	smooth muscles
digestive system	triceps

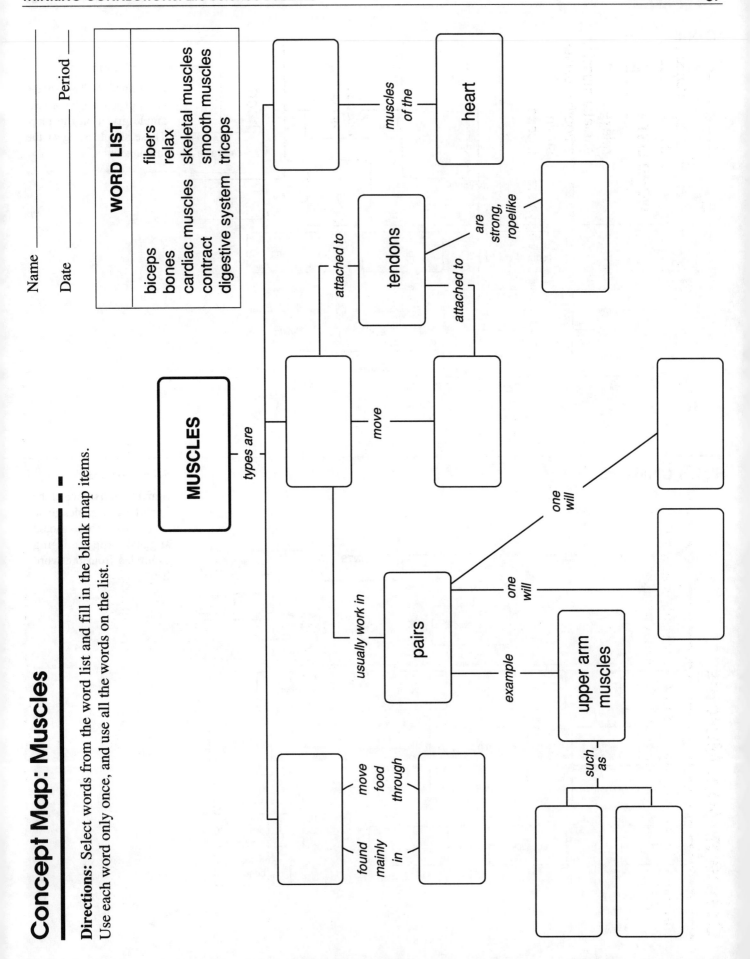

MUSCLES

types are

muscles of the — heart

attached to — tendons — *are strong, ropelike*

attached to

move

usually work in — pairs

one will

one will

example — upper arm muscles

such as

found mainly in

move food through

Concept Map: Muscles

Directions: Select words from the word list and fill in the blank map items. Use each word only once, and use all the words on the list.

Name ——————

Date ——————

Period ——————

WORD LIST

biceps	relaxes
bones	skeletal muscles
cardiac muscles	smooth muscles
contracts	strain
digestive system	triceps
fibers	

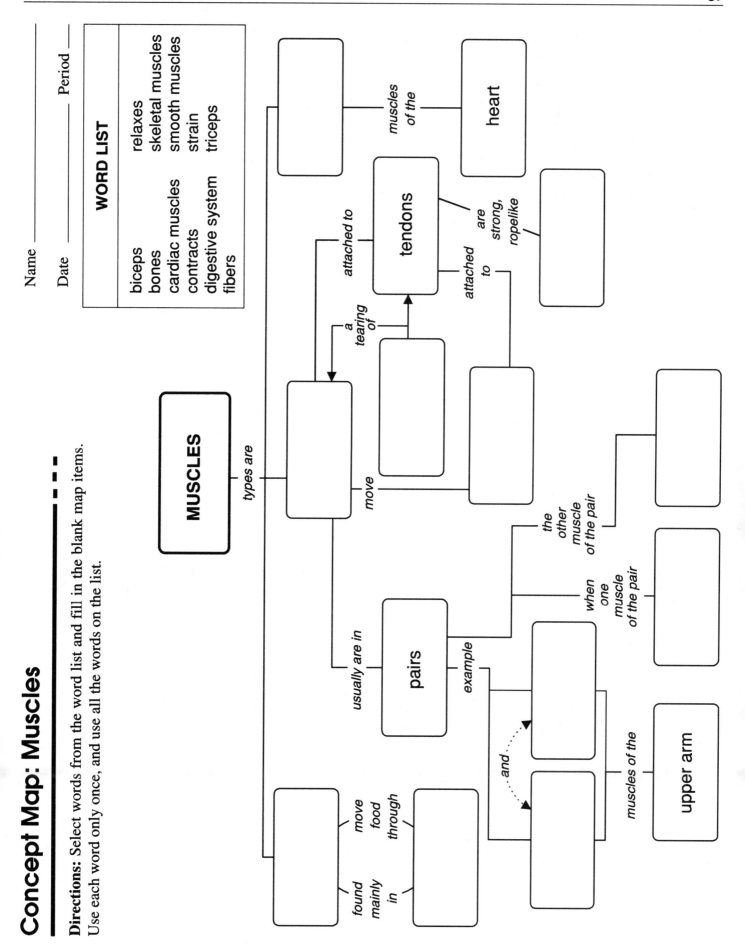

Critical Thinking ⟶  C NCEPT FILE

Muscles

Types of Muscles

There are three kinds of muscles in the human body:

Cardiac muscles	Smooth muscles	Skeletal muscles
These are the muscles of the heart.	These are the muscles that act automatically. Most are found in the digestive system. They move food through the system.	These are the muscles that move bones. They usually occur in pairs. When one muscle contracts, the other one in the pair relaxes. Examples would be the biceps and the triceps of the upper arm.

Vocabulary

❏ **strain**—the tearing of tendons and skeletal muscles

❏ **tendons**—strong, ropelike fibers that connect skeletal muscles to bones

MUSCLES

Lower Challenge

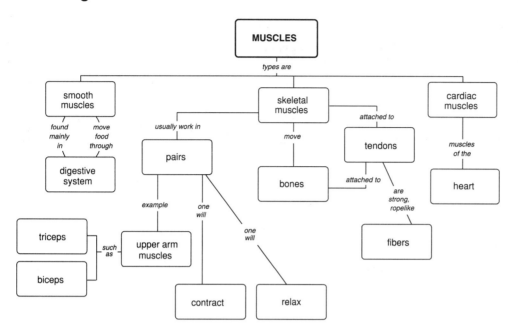

Score: 10 words

Starting hints: The item on the lower left, *upper arm muscles*, points to biceps and triceps (in either order).

The item *tendons* (center right) refers to ropelike fibers that are attached to bones and skeletal muscles.

The item on the extreme right, *heart*, points to cardiac muscles.

Higher Challenge

Score: 11 words
Starting hints: See notes above.

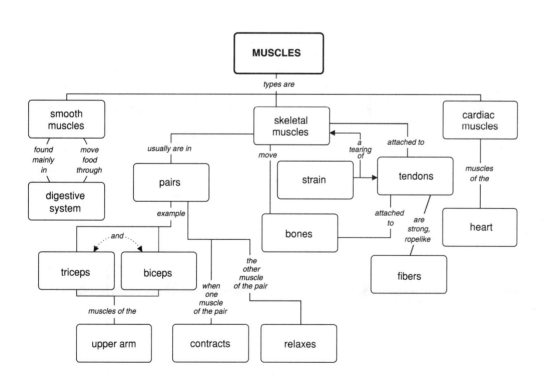

Name _____

Period _____

Date _____

Concept Map: The Heart

Directions: Select words from the word list to fill in the blank map items. Use each word only once, and use all the words on the list.

WORD LIST

arteries
blood
body
left ventricle
lungs
muscle
oxygen
right atrium
valves
veins

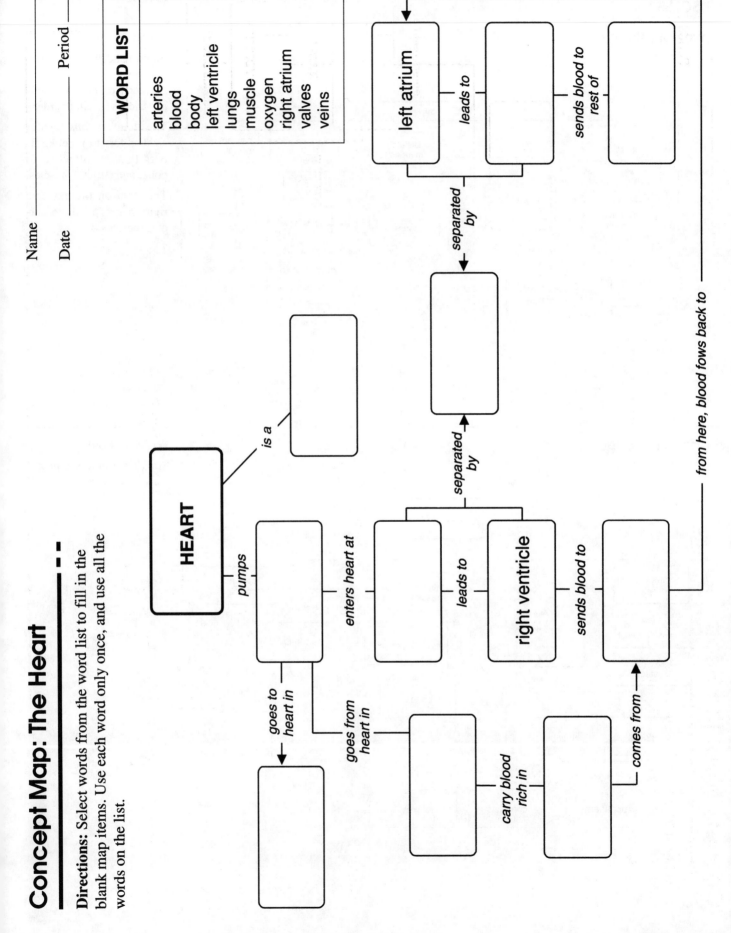

Concept Map: The Heart

Directions: Select words from the word list to fill in the blank map items. Use each word only once, and use all the words on the list.

Name _____

Date _____

Period _____

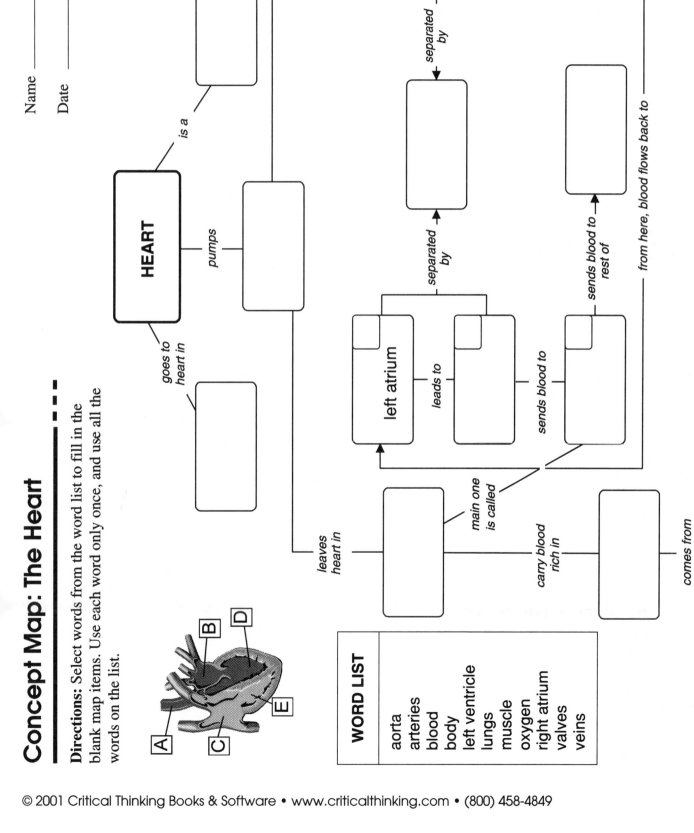

WORD LIST

aorta
arteries
blood
body
left ventricle
lungs
muscle
oxygen
right atrium
valves
veins

Critical Thinking

The Heart

Function

- the heart is a special muscle of the body
- the heart pumps blood throughout the body

Parts

- left atrium—receives blood from the lungs, sends it to left ventricle
- left ventricle—pumps blood from left atrium into aorta, then to rest of body
- right atrium—receives blood from the body, sends it to heart through right ventricle
- right ventricle—pumps blood from right atrium to lungs
- valves—doorways between the chambers of the heart that keep blood flowing only one way

Vocabulary

- ❏ **aorta**—the main artery of the heart, leading blood to the rest of the body
- ❏ **artery**—a tube that leads oxygen-rich blood away from the heart
- ❏ **atrium**—an upper chamber of the heart
- ❏ **lungs**—give blood oxygen
- ❏ **vein**—a tube that leads blood to the heart
- ❏ **ventricle**—a lower chamber of the heart

THE HEART

Lower Challenge

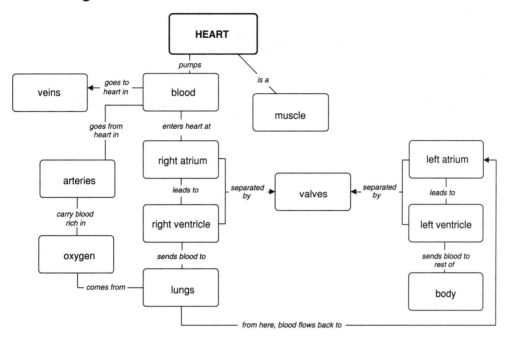

Score: 10

Starting hints: The seed words *left atrium* and *right ventricle* should point to *left ventricle* and *right atrium*, respectively. The connector *pumps* at top suggests *blood*. The connector *sends blood to rest of* suggests *body*.

Higher Challenge

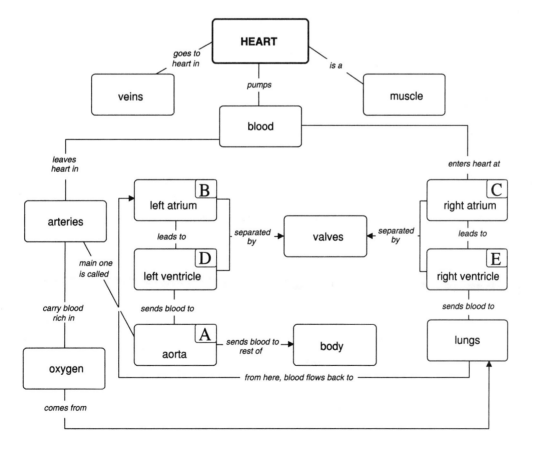

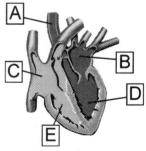

Score: 16 (11 words and 5 letters)

Starting hints: See above.

Diagram Key:

A   aorta
B   left atrium
C   right atrium
D   left ventricle
E   right ventricle

Concept Map: Digestive System

Name _____

Date _____ Period ____

Directions: Select words from the word list to fill in the blank map items. Use each word only once, and use all the words on the list.

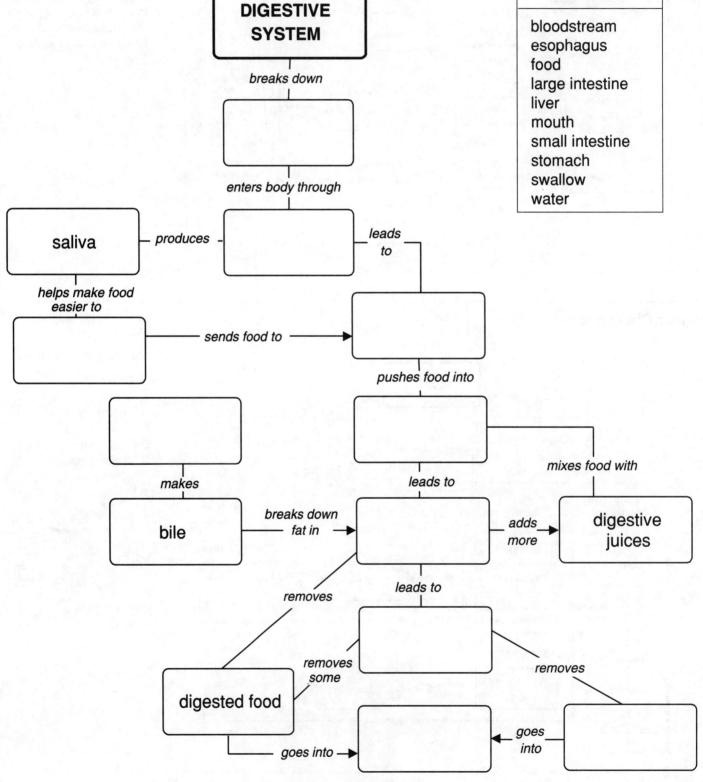

WORD LIST

- bloodstream
- esophagus
- food
- large intestine
- liver
- mouth
- small intestine
- stomach
- swallow
- water

Concept Map: Digestive System

Name _____

Date _____ Period ____

Directions: Select words from the word list to fill in the blank map items. Use each word only once, and use all the words on the list. In the small boxes, write the letters that match parts of the diagram.

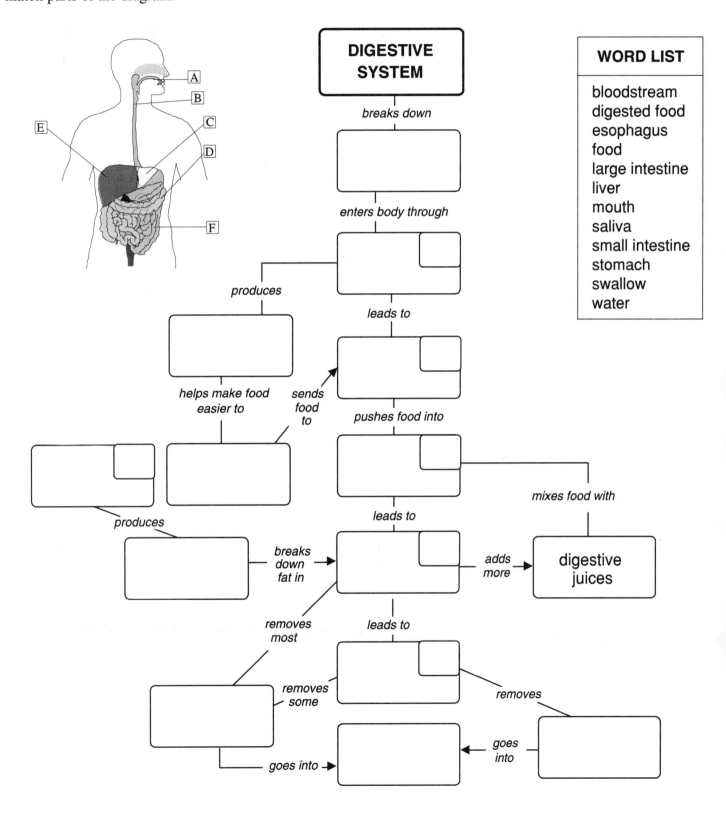

WORD LIST

bloodstream
digested food
esophagus
food
large intestine
liver
mouth
saliva
small intestine
stomach
swallow
water

Critical Thinking → C💡NCEPT FILE

Digestive System

Function	Vocabulary
The digestive system breaks down food into a form that the body can use. It has five main parts.	☐ **bile**—a green liquid that breaks up large fat droplets into small fat droplets ☐ **esophagus**—the tube that connects the mouth to the stomach

Mouth

- place where food enters the body
- makes saliva, which helps make food easier to swallow

Small Intestine

- removes most of the digested food, sending it into the bloodstream
- adds more digestive juices to the food
- leads to the large intestine

Stomach

- mixes food with digestive juices
- opens into the small intestine

Liver

- helps digest fat
- produces bile

Large Intestine

- removes some of the digested food
- removes water from the food
- send water and food into the bloodstream

DIGESTIVE SYSTEM

Lower Challenge

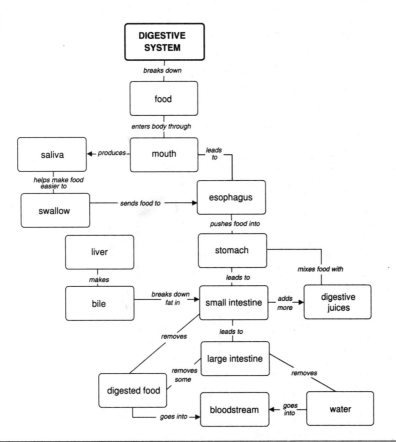

Score: 10 words

Starting hints: The seed item *saliva* on the upper left points back to mouth. The seed item *bile* points back to liver.

The seed item *digestive juices* suggests stomach.

Higher Challenge

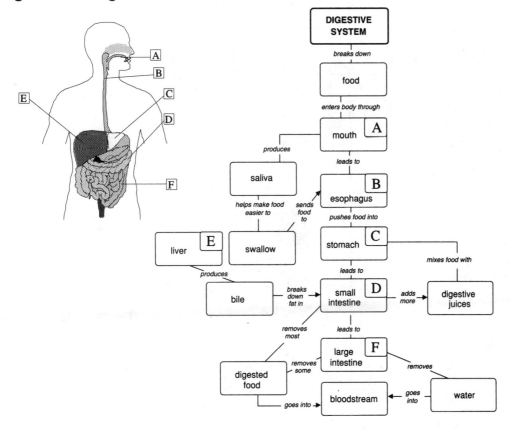

Score: 12 words

Starting hints: See notes above.

Diagram Key:

A   mouth
B   esophagus
C   stomach
D   small intestine
E   liver
F   large intestine

Concept Map: Biomes

Name _____

Date _____   Period _____

Directions: Select words from the word list and fill in the blank map items.
Use each word only once, and use all the words on the list.

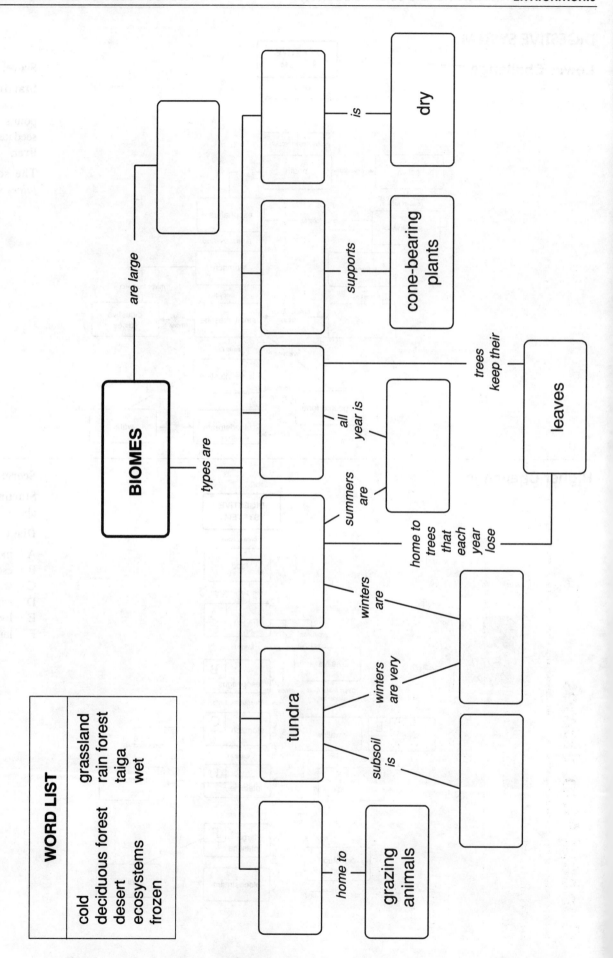

WORD LIST

cold	grassland
deciduous forest	rain forest
desert	taiga
ecosystems	wet
frozen	

Concept Map: Biomes

Directions: Select words from the word list and fill in the blank map items.
Use each word only once, and use all the words on the list.

WORD LIST

coffee tree	rain forest
cold	taiga
conifers	tundra
deciduous forest	wet
deciduous trees	
desert	
ecosystems	
grassland	
grazing animals	
leaves	

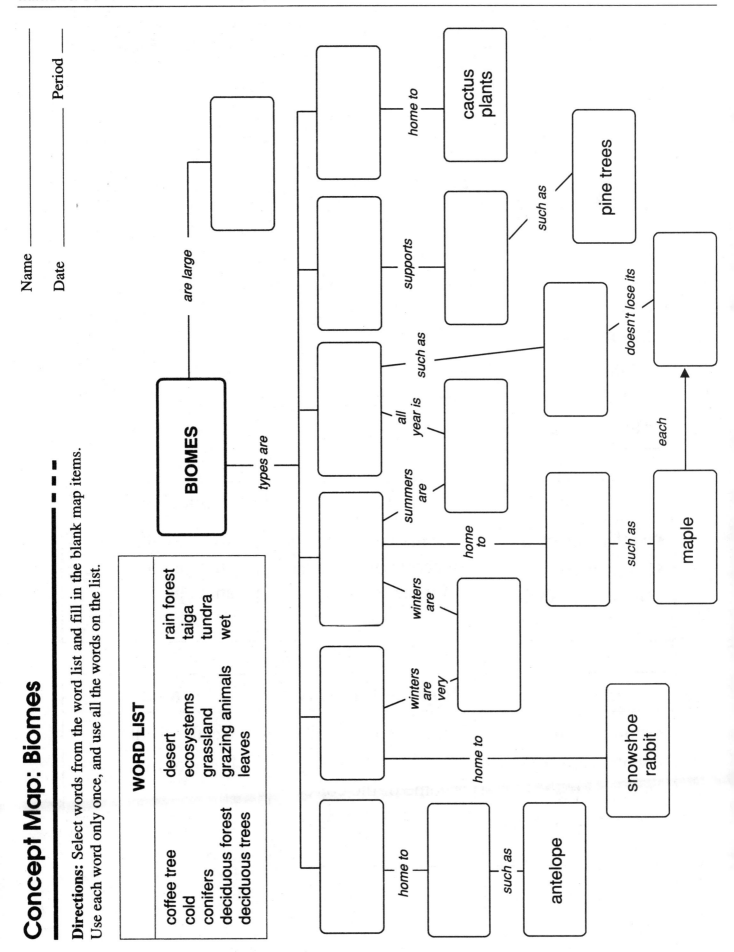

Critical Thinking → C💡NCEPT FILE

Biomes

Types

Biomes are large ecosystems. Each has a distinct climate and certain types of plants and animals.

They include:

- taiga
- tropical rain forest
- desert
- deciduous forest
- tundra
- grassland

Vocabulary

☐ **deciduous**—a plant that loses its leaves each year

☐ **ecosystem**—a community's interaction with its physical environment

Tundra

- winters are cold
- home of the snowshoe rabbit

Taiga

- main plants are cone-bearing plants, such as pine trees

Grassland

- home to grazing animals, such as the antelope

Deciduous Forest

- summers are wet
- winters are cold
- home of the deciduous tree, like the maple

Tropical Rain Forest

- weather is wet all year
- home of the coffee tree (not deciduous)

Desert

- weather is dry
- home of the cactus

BIOMES

Lower Challenge

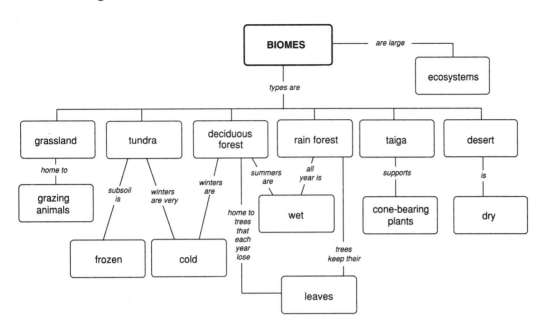

Score: 10 words

Starting hints: The item *dry* on the lower right suggests desert. The seed item *grazing animals* suggests grassland.

Higher Challenge

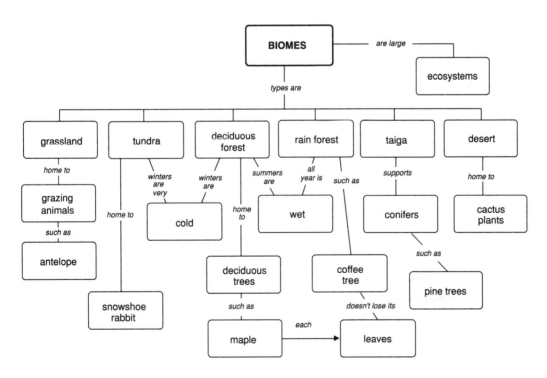

Score: 15 words

Starting hints: Start with the seed items *pine trees* to point up to conifers and taiga, and *antelope* to point up to grazing animals and grassland.

Concept Map: Fresh-water Ecosystems

Name _____

Date _____

Period _____

Directions: Select words from the word list and fill in the blank map items. Use each word only once, and use all the words on the list.

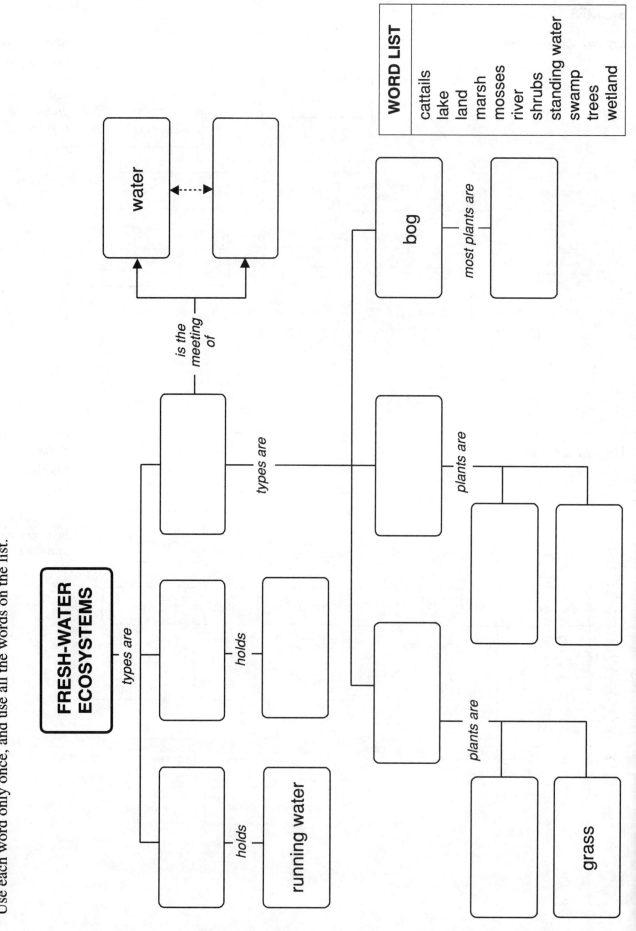

WORD LIST

cattails
lake
land
marsh
mosses
river
shrubs
standing water
swamp
trees
wetland

FRESH-WATER ECOSYSTEMS

types are

holds

holds

running water

types are

is the meeting of

water

plants are

plants are

grass

bog

most plants are

Concept Map: Fresh-water Ecosystems

Directions: Select words from the word list and fill in the blank map items. Use each word only once, and use all the words on the list.

© 2001 Critical Thinking Books & Software • www.criticalthinking.com • (800) 458-4849   153

Name _____

Date _____ Period _____

WORD LIST

bog	mosses
cranberries	river
grass	running water
lake	shrubs
marsh	standing water
swamp	
trees	
water	
wetland	

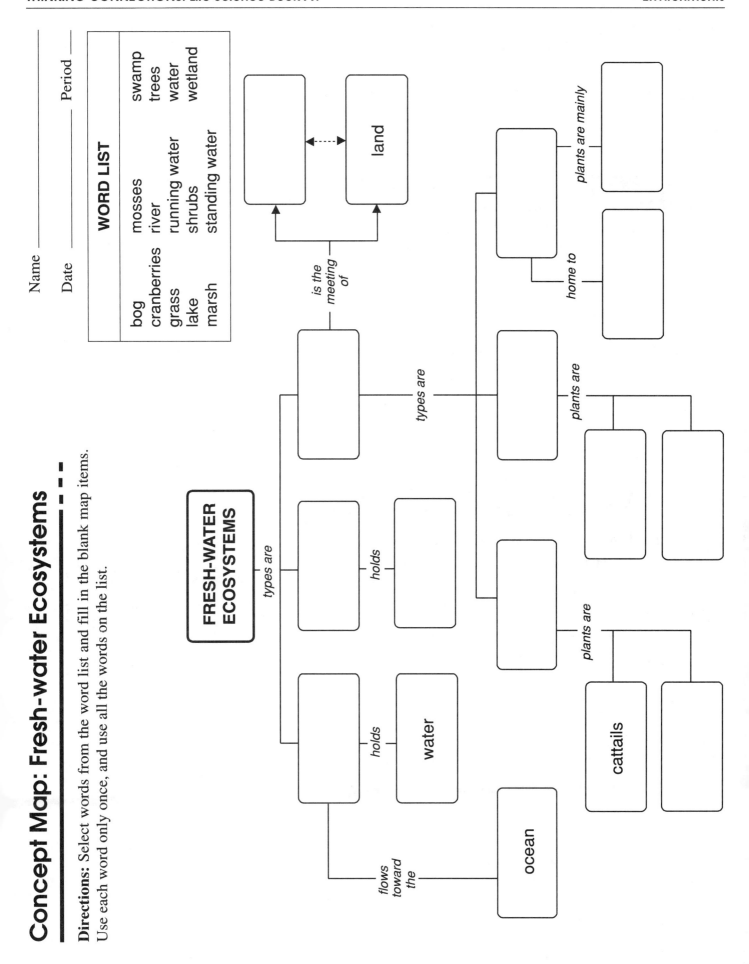

FRESH-WATER ECOSYSTEMS

is the meeting of

land

types are

types are

holds

holds

water

flows toward the

ocean

plants are mainly

home to

plants are

plants are

cattails

Critical Thinking →

Fresh-water Ecosystems

Types

There are three main types of fresh-water ecosystems.

Lakes	**Rivers**	**Wetlands**

• hold standing water	• hold running water
	• flow to the ocean
		• are the meeting of water and land
		• three main types:
		  – swamp: has trees and shrubs
		  – marsh: home to cattails and grasses
		  – bog: most plants are mosses, also home to cranberries

Vocabulary

❒ **standing water**—water that does not flow

FRESH-WATER ECOSYSTEMS

Lower Challenge

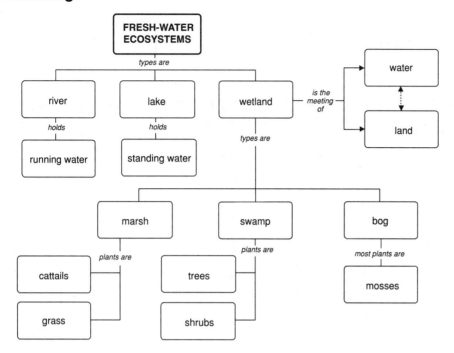

Score: 7 words

Starting hints: The seed item *bog* points to the wetlands. The seed item *running water* suggests river.

Higher Challenge

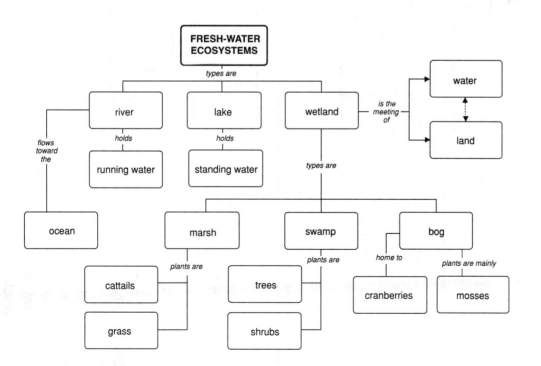

Score: 10 words

Starting hints: The seed item *cattails* points to marsh. The seed item *ocean* suggests river above.

Concept Map: Saltwater Ecosystems

Name ———————————————

Date ———————————   Period ———

Directions: Select words from the word list and fill in the blank map items.
Use each word only once, and use all the words on the list.

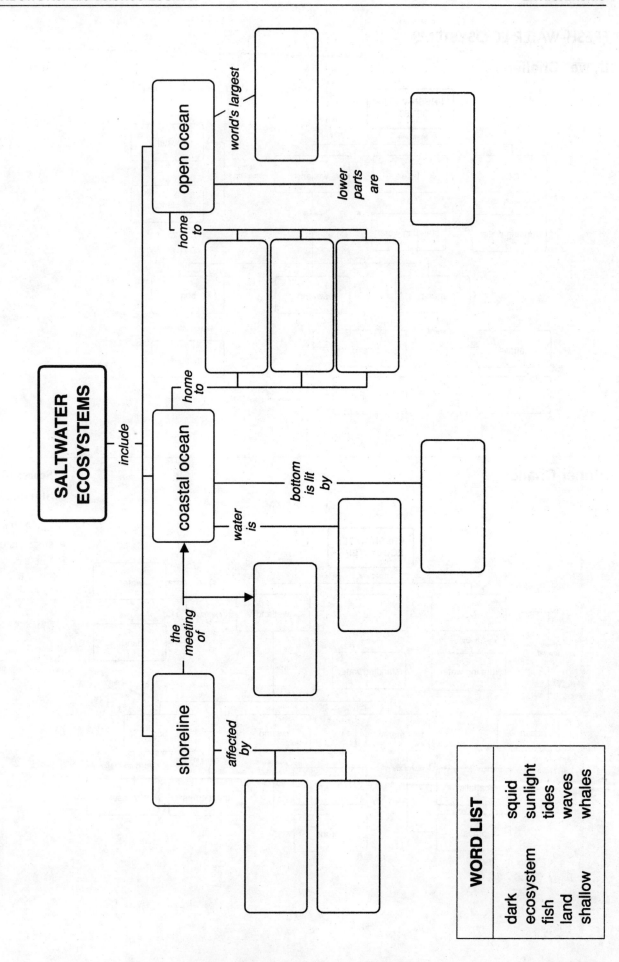

SALTWATER ECOSYSTEMS

include

open ocean

world's largest

lower parts are

home to

coastal ocean

home to

bottom is lit by

water is

the meeting of

shoreline

affected by

WORD LIST

dark	squid
ecosystem	sunlight
fish	tides
land	waves
shallow	whales

Concept Map: Saltwater Ecosystems

Directions: Select words from the word list and fill in the blank map items. Use each word only once, and use all the words on the list.

Name —————————————

Date ————————————— Period ————

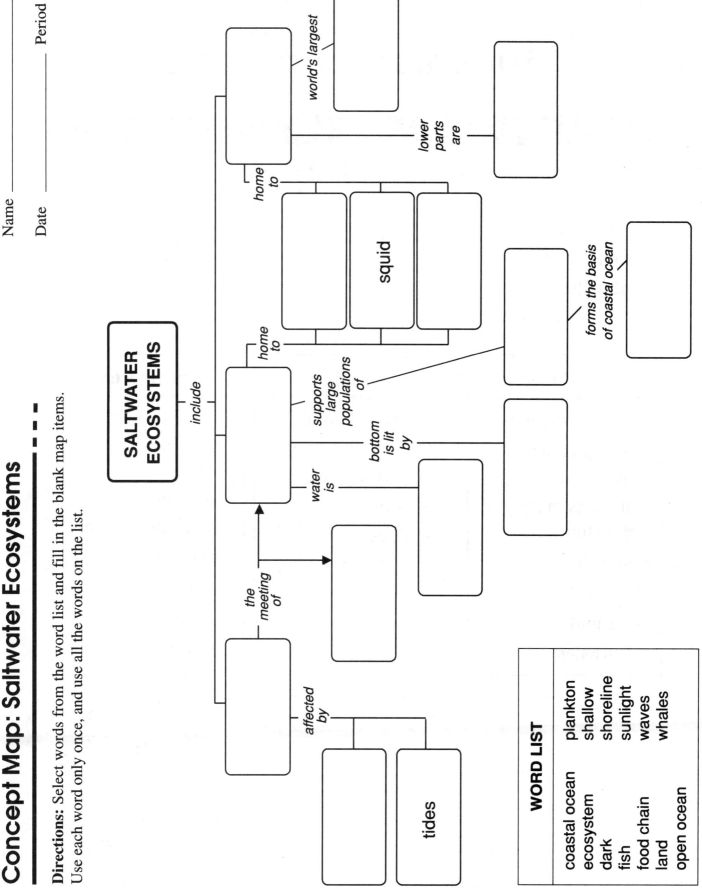

SALTWATER ECOSYSTEMS

include

home to — *world's largest*

lower parts are

home to — squid

supports large populations of — *forms the basis of coastal ocean*

water is — *bottom is lit by*

the meeting of

affected by — tides

WORD LIST

coastal ocean	plankton
ecosystem	shallow
dark	shoreline
fish	sunlight
food chain	waves
land	whales
open ocean	

Critical Thinking → C☼NCEPT FILE

Saltwater Ecosystems

Types	Vocabulary
There are three basic types of saltwater ecosystems: • open ocean • coastal ocean • shoreline	❑ **plankton**—microscopic life of the ocean that forms the start of food chains

Coastal Ocean	Shoreline	Open Ocean

• water is shallow
• sunlight reaches the bottom
• supports many plankton
• home to
  – fish
  – squid
  – whales
	• is where coastal ocean and land meet
	• is affected by
	  – waves
	  – tides
		• is the largest ecosystem in the world
		• sunlight does not reach the bottom
		• home to
		  – fish
		  – squid
		  – whales

SALTWATER ECOSYSTEMS

Lower Challenge

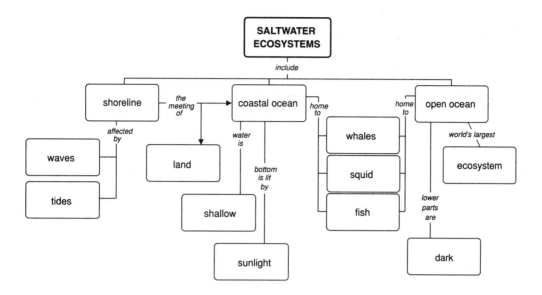

Score: 10 words

Starting hints: The connector *the meeting of* between shoreline and coastal ocean suggests *land*.

The seed item *open ocean* and connector *world's largest* suggest *ecosystem*.

Higher Challenge

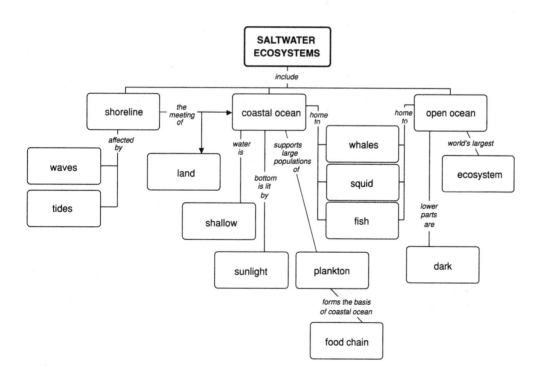

Score: 13 words

Starting hints: The seed item *tides* pairs with *waves*.

The seed item *squid* suggests whales and fish, in either order.

Name _____

Date _____

Period _____

Concept Map: The Water Cycle

Directions: Select words from the word list and fill in the blank map items. Use each word only once, and use all the words on the list.

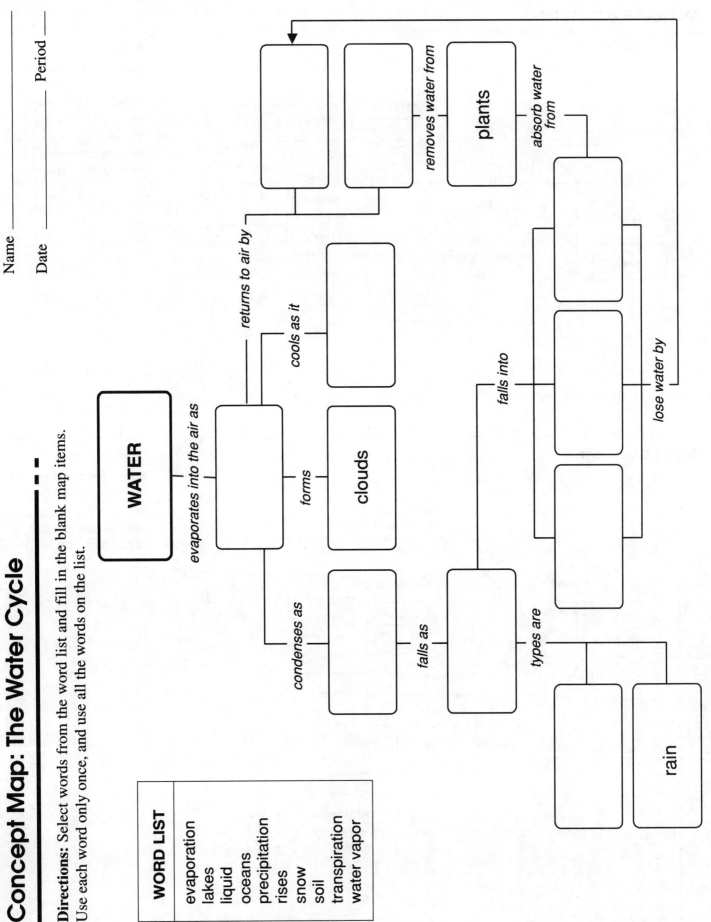

WORD LIST

evaporation
lakes
liquid
oceans
precipitation
rises
snow
soil
transpiration
water vapor

Concept Map: The Water Cycle

Directions: Select words from the word list and fill in the blank map items.
Use each word only once, and use all the words on the list.

Name ——————————

Date ——————————

Period ——————————

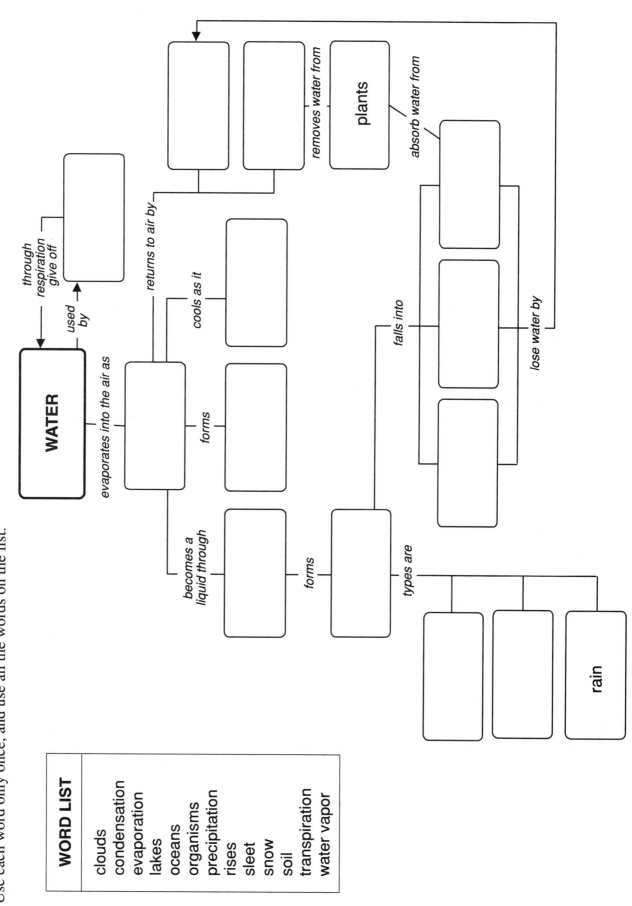

WORD LIST

clouds
condensation
evaporation
lakes
oceans
organisms
precipitation
rises
sleet
snow
soil
transpiration
water vapor

Critical Thinking →  CONCEPT FILE

Water Cycle

Water Vapor

Water exists in the air as water vapor.

Water vapor
- cools as it rises
- forms clouds

Liquid Water

Water returns to the earth as
- rain
- snow
- sleet

Water falls onto
- soil
- oceans
- lakes

Water is used by organisms. Organisms give off water through the process of respiration.

Vocabulary

❑ **condensation**—the forming of liquid water as water vapor cools

❑ **evaporation**—the change of water from a liquid to a vapor, returning water to the air

❑ **transpiration**—the loss of water from plants

THE WATER CYCLE

Lower Challenge

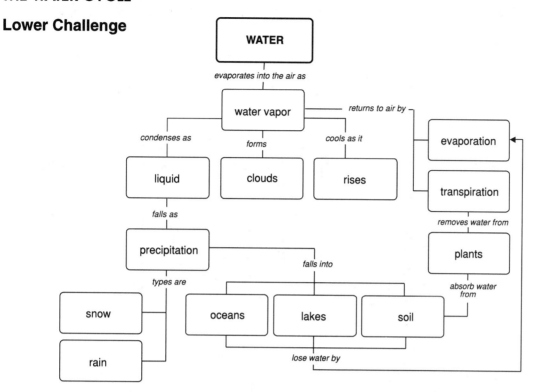

Score: 10 words

Starting hints: The combination of the connector and item on the right, removes *water from plants*, points to transpiration.

On the lower left, the pair to *rain* is snow.

Higher Challenge

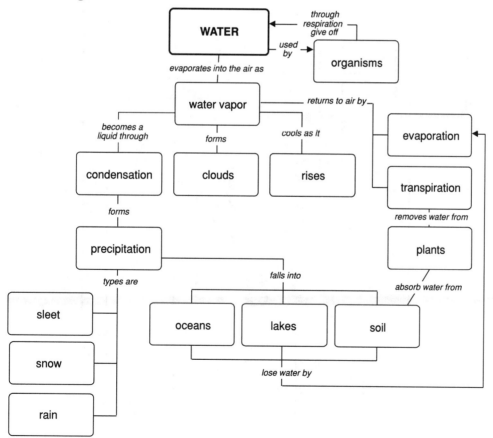

Score: 13 words

Starting hints: The combination of the connector and item on the right, *removes water from plants*, points to transpiration.

On the lower left, the matching items to *rain* are *snow* and *sleet*, in either order.

Concept Map: The Nitrogen Cycle

Name _____

Period _____

Date _____

Directions: Select words from the word list and fill in the blank map items.
Use each word only once, and use all the words on the list.

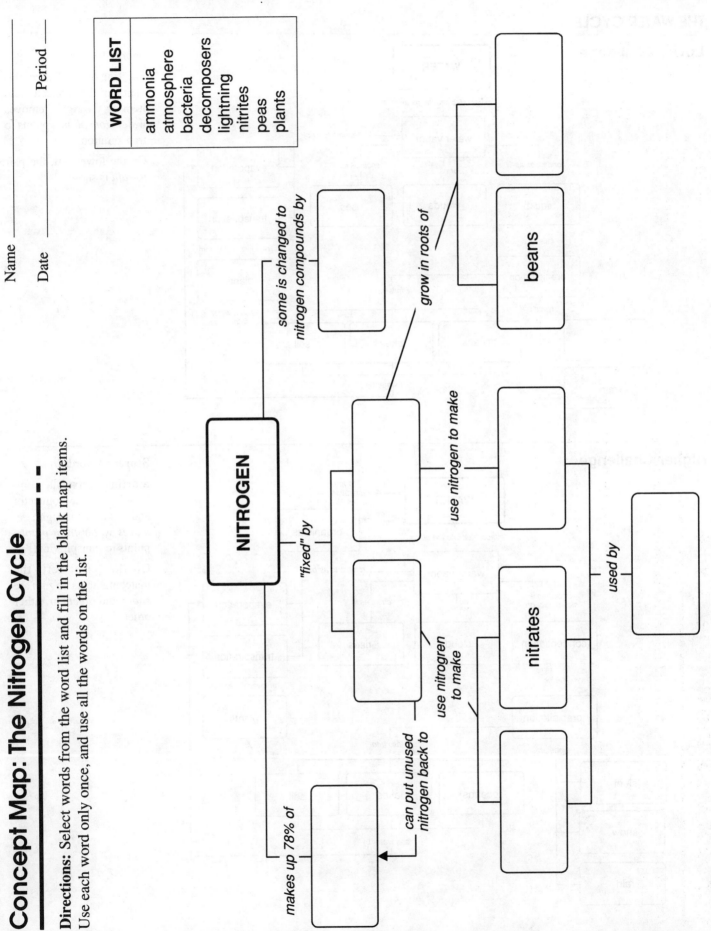

Concept Map: The Nitrogen Cycle

Name ——————

Date —————— Period ——————

Directions: Select words from the word list and fill in the blank map items. Use each word only once, and use all the words on the list.

WORD LIST

ammonia
animals
atmosphere
bacteria
beans
building blocks
decomposers
lightning
nitrites
peas
plants

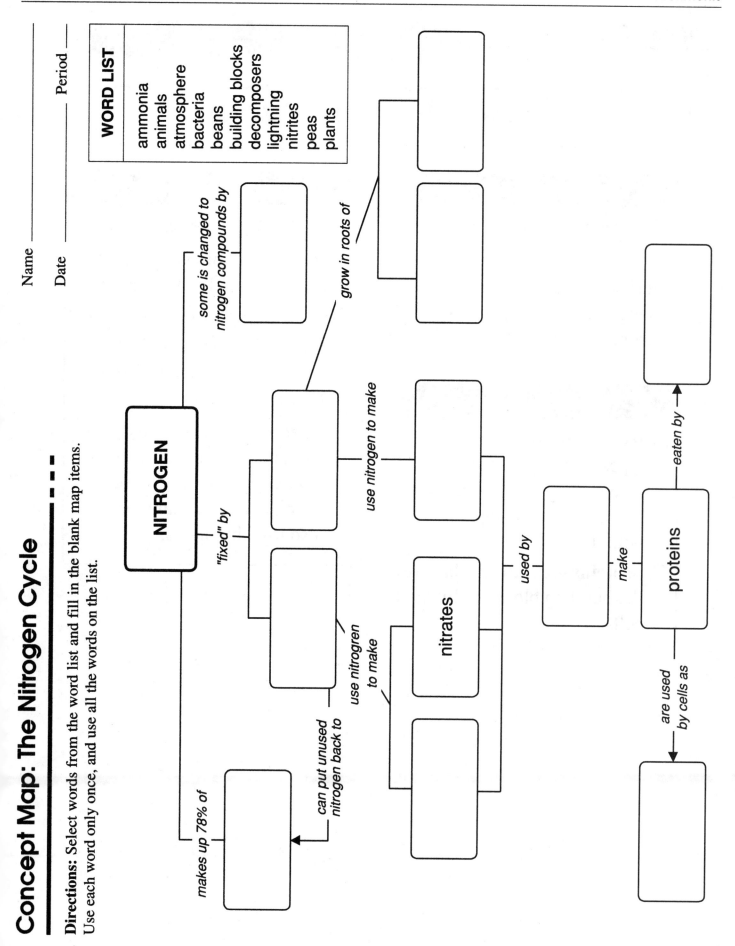

Critical Thinking → C NCEPT FILE

The Nitrogen Cycle

Nitrogen in our Air

Nitrogen makes up 78% of our air.

During storms, lightning changes some nitrogen into nitrogen compounds.

Vocabulary

- ❏ **fixing nitrogen**—certain types of living things can take nitrogen out of the air and make new compounds with it

- ❏ **proteins**—chemicals that are the building blocks of living cells

Living Things Use Nitrogen

All living things need nitrogen.

Certain living things can "fix" nitrogen. These living things are:

- decomposers—these use nitrogen to make nitrates and nitrites, which are used by plants to make proteins

- bacteria—these organisms live and grow in the roots of peas and beans. They use nitrogen to make ammonia, also used by plants.

THE NITROGEN CYCLE

Lower Challenge

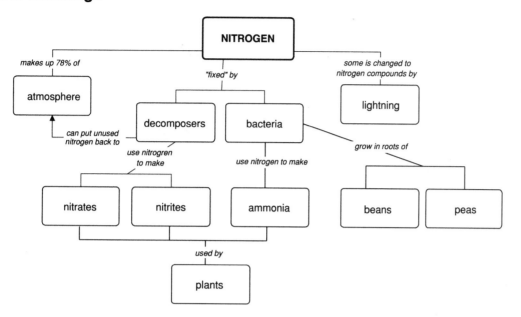

Score: 10 words

Starting hints: The connector *grow in roots of* should suggest the item *peas*.

The seed *nitrates* should suggest its pair to the left, *nitrites*. The use of the term *fixed by* in the central connector suggests bacteria and decomposers.

Higher Challenge

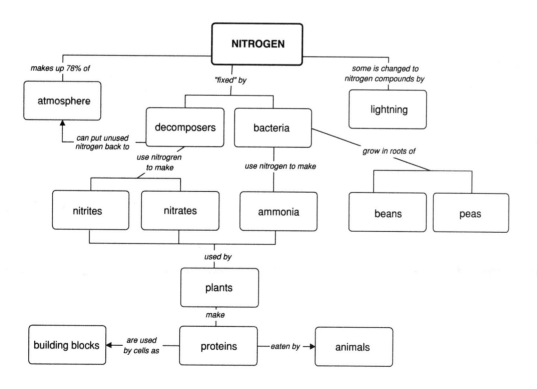

Score: 11 words

Starting hints: Start with seed item *proteins* to get to *building blocks* and *animals*. The connector *grow in roots of* should suggest the items *beans* and *peas*.

The seed *nitrates* should suggest its pair to the left, *nitrites*. The use of the term *fixed by* in the central connector suggests bacteria and decomposers.

Concept Map: The Oxygen/Carbon Dioxide Cycle

Name _____

Date _____

Period _____

Directions: Select words from the word list and fill in the blank map items.
Use each word only once, and use all the words on the list.

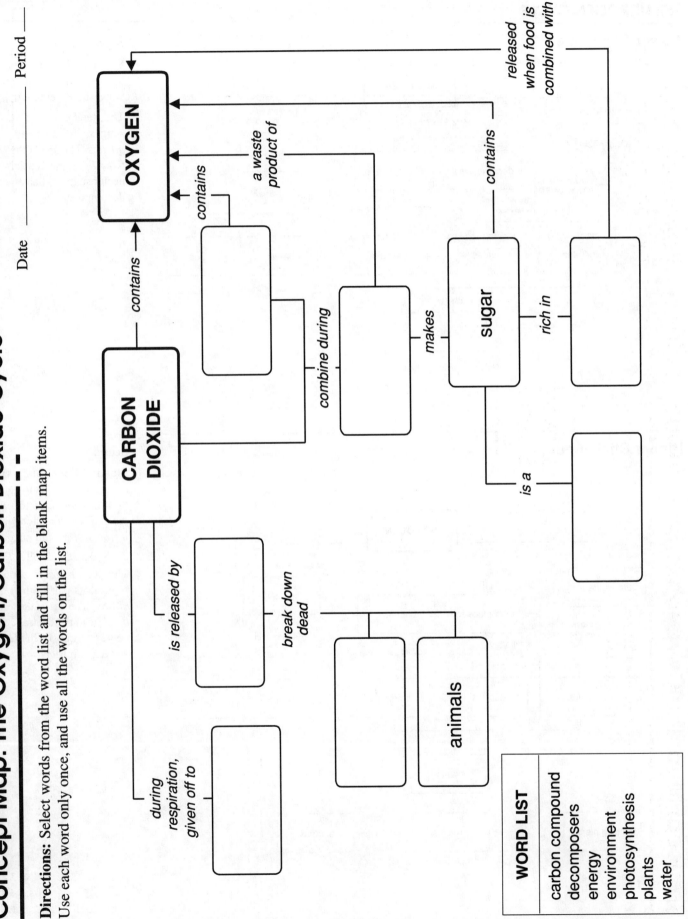

WORD LIST

carbon compound
decomposers
energy
environment
photosynthesis
plants
water

Name _____

Date _____

Period _____

Concept Map: The Oxygen/Carbon Dioxide Cycle

Directions: Select words from the word list and fill in the blank map items. Use each word only once, and use all the words on the list.

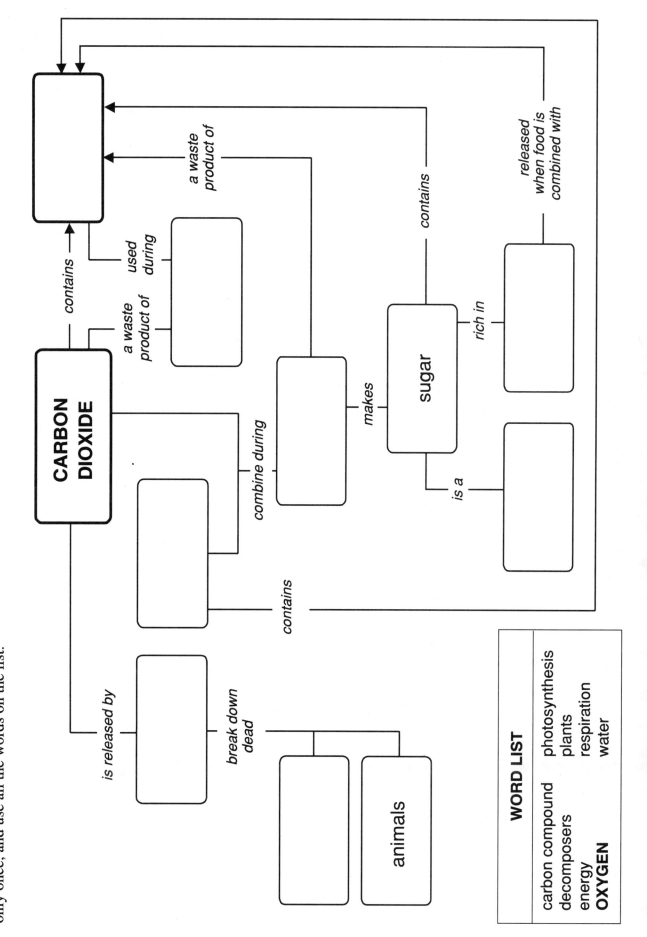

WORD LIST

carbon compound	photosynthesis
decomposers	plants
energy	respiration
OXYGEN	water

CARBON DIOXIDE

contains

a waste product of

used during

a waste product of

combine during

makes

sugar

contains

rich in

is a

released when food is combined with

contains

is released by

break down dead

animals

Critical Thinking →

The Oxygen/Carbon Dioxide Cycle

Oxygen

- is used during respiration to burn food
- is a waste product of photosynthesis

Carbon Dioxide

- combines with water during photosynthesis
- released by decomposers when they break down dead plants and animals
- is a waste product of respiration

Vocabulary

- ☐ **photosynthesis**—the process by which plants combine water and carbon dioxide to make sugar, a compound containing carbon and oxygen, and rich in energy
- ☐ **respiration**—the process by which an organism exchanges gases with its environment

THE OXYGEN/CARBON DIOXIDE CYCLE

Lower Challenge

Score: 7 words

Starting hints: The connector *makes* points to *photosynthesis* above it.

The connector *break down dead* suggests *decomposers* above it.

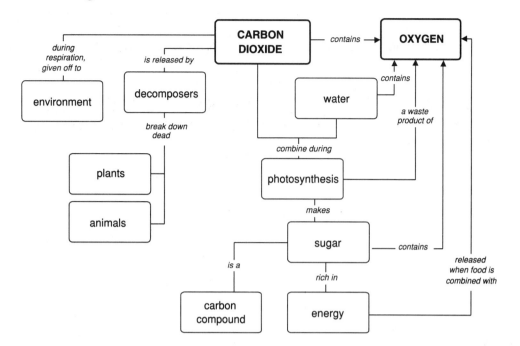

Higher Challenge

Score: 11 words

Starting hints: See notes above.

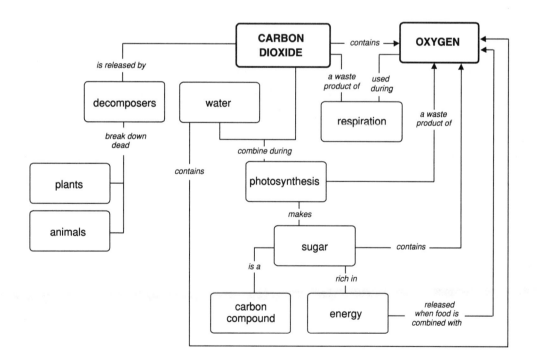

THINKING CONNECTIONS B1
SAMPLE ACTIVITY

Thinking Connections Life Science Book B1 is a continuation of the skills learned in Book A1. The B1 book is for grades 7–12. Many of the concepts in Book A1 are also examined in Book B1 but in greater detail. On the next four pages you will find the following samples from Thinking Connections B1:

- a Lower Challenge concept map
- a Higher Challenge concept map
- a Concept File
- an answer page for both concept maps

Concept Map: Cell Structures

Directions: Select words from the word list and fill in the blank map items.
Use each word only once, and use all the words on the list.

Name _____

Date _____

Period _____

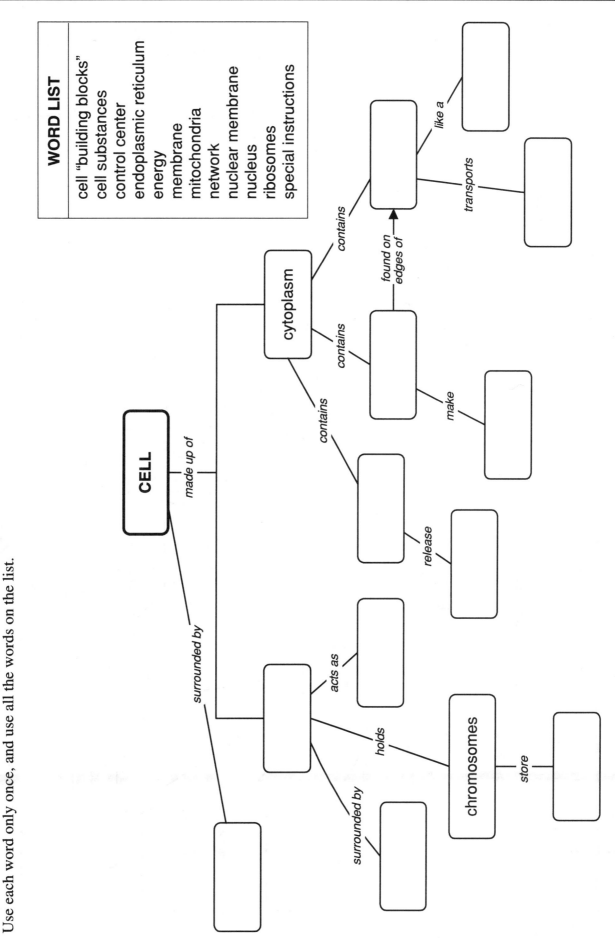

Concept Map: Cell Structures

Directions: Select words from the word list and fill in the blank map items. Use each word only once, and use all the words on the list. Then use two different highlighters, colored pencils, or crayons to color in items that are (1) strictly related to plants and (2) are related to both plants and animals. Show your color scheme in the legend.

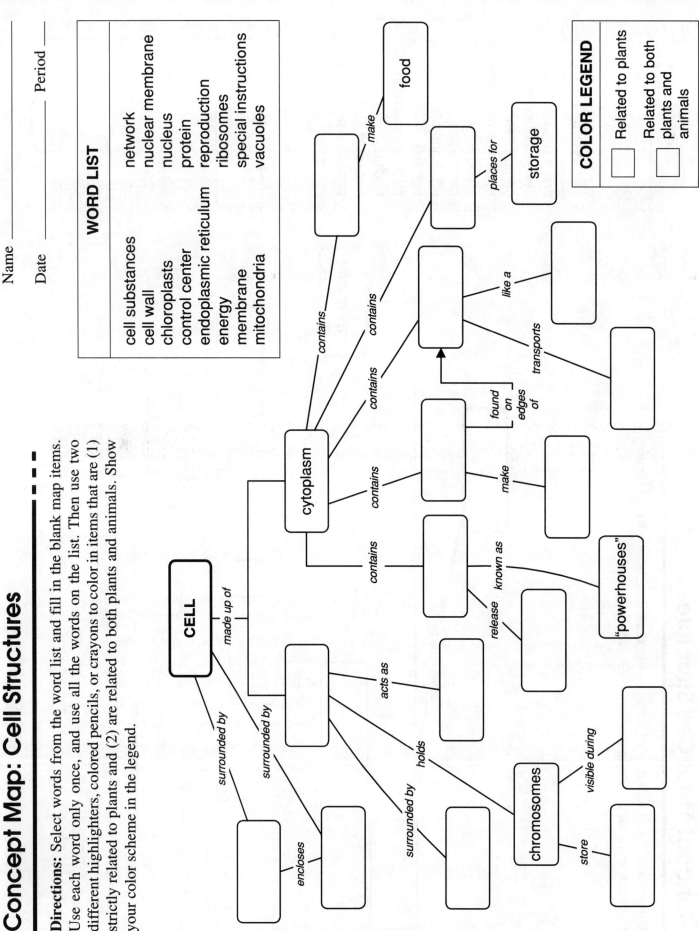

WORD LIST

cell substances	network
cell wall	nuclear membrane
chloroplasts	nucleus
control center	protein
endoplasmic reticulum	reproduction
energy	ribosomes
membrane	special instructions
mitochondria	vacuoles

COLOR LEGEND

☐ Related to plants

☐ Related to both plants and animals

Critical Thinking

Cell Structures

Background

Cells

- are the basic units of living things
- are protected by a membrane
- are also protected by a tough outer wall (plant cells)

Vocabulary

Check your understanding—these terms are explained on this page.

- ❏ **chromosomes**
- ❏ **cytoplasm**
- ❏ **endoplasmic reticulum**
- ❏ **membrane**
- ❏ **nuclear membrane**
- ❏ **nucleus**
- ❏ **protein**
- ❏ **ribosomes**
- ❏ **vacuole**

Two Main Areas of the Cell

Nucleus

The nucleus

- is surrounded by a nuclear membrane
- is the control center of the cell
- stores special cell information in chromosomes, tiny threadlike structures seen during cell reproduction

Cytoplasm

The cytoplasm is the place of many cell activities and structures.

- Mitochondria are the "powerhouses," storing energy.
- The "building blocks" of cells (proteins) are manufactured by ribosomes (located along the endoplasmic reticulum).
- Cell substances are transported on a network called the endoplasmic reticulum.
- Plant cells have vacuoles in which cell materials are stored.
- Food is made in the chloroplasts of plant cells.

Cell Structures
LOWER CHALLENGE

Score: 12 words

Starting hints: The connector *found on the edges of* is a good early clue. In addition, note that something *holds* chromosomes.

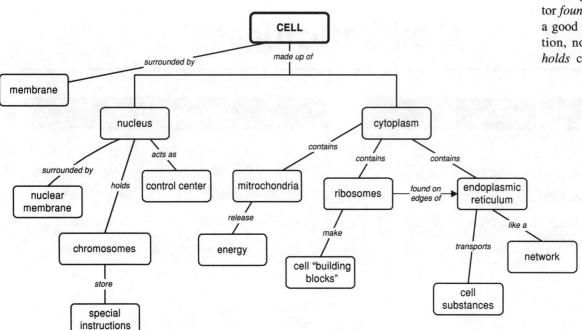

HIGHER CHALLENGE

Score: 38 (16 words + 22 colored boxes)

Starting hints: The connector *found on the edges of* is a good early clue. In addition, note that something *holds* chromosomes.

Notes: Plant-cell features are additions to this level.

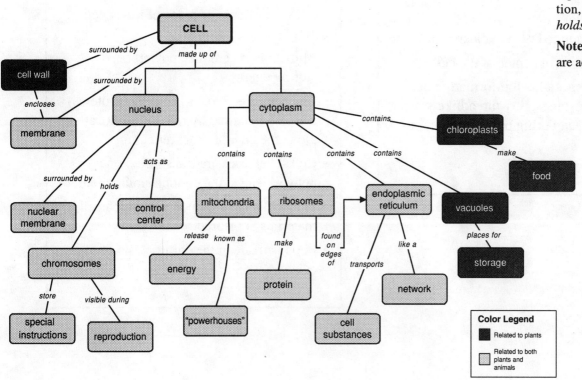